MURDEROUS MINDS AUSTRALIA

MURDEROUS MINDS AUSTRALIA

International Serial Killers Encyclopedia

Book 5

ALAN R. WARREN

House of Mystery Publishing

Seattle, Washington, USA

Vancouver, British Columbia, Canada

First Edition

ISBN (Paperback): 978-1-989980-94-1
ISBN (eBook): 978-1-989980-95-8

Cover design, formatting, layout, and editing by Evening Sky Publishing Services

Contents

Book Description

The *International Serial Killers Encyclopedia* series sheds light on the murderous minds of many killers, including their motivations, methods, and madness, through detailed research and explicit retelling of events. Some are notorious names that echo through history books, while others are lesser-known killers whose stories are no less harrowing. Each volume reveals a new layer of darkness.

Australia is known for its breathtaking landscapes, exotic wildlife, and laid-back culture—but a darker side lurks beneath the surface of this serene country. *Murderous Minds Australia*, the fifth volume in Alan R. Warren's acclaimed series, uncovers the chilling stories of some of the most notorious serial killers ever to walk on Australian soil. From the harsh outback to bustling cities, Australia has witnessed crimes so horrifying they have scarred the national consciousness.

This volume examines the lives and deeds of killers who have shattered the peace of this distant land and unearths the grim details of Australia's darkest crimes. You will find infamous cases that have gained international attention and lesser-known but equally terrifying stories. *Murderous Minds Australia* is a comprehensive guide to the country's most notorious serial killers.

Prepare yourself for a compelling and unsettling journey through Australia's criminal history as Alan R. Warren brings to life the harrowing tales of the murderous minds in Australia.

Introduction

In this fifth volume of the *International Serial Killers Encyclopedia*, titled *Murderous Minds Australia*, we venture into the "Land Down Under," uncovering a side of Australia far from its sun-drenched beaches and picturesque landscapes. Australia, a nation known for its vibrant culture and rich natural beauty, has not been immune to the presence of individuals capable of extreme violence. Within the shadows of this vast and remote continent, many chilling and unfathomable crimes have taken place—acts committed by some of the most notorious and brutal serial killers in history. The isolation of some of its regions and the complexity of its cities have provided a unique backdrop for horrific events that continue to haunt its national consciousness.

From notorious bushland murders to gruesome urban killings, *Murderous Minds Australia* delves deep into the psyches of those responsible while examining the social and psychological factors that may have contributed to their chilling behavior. This book presents a masterful account of these dark figures. It offers an unflinching exploration of each case, revealing the details of the crimes and the complex investigative processes that followed. As in the previous volumes, his thorough research and insightful storytelling allow readers to fully grasp the scale and severity of each killer's actions.

True crime enthusiasts will be riveted and horrified by the twisted accounts within these pages. Warren not only tells the stories of the killers but also delves into the psychological and social factors that may have contributed to their actions. In doing so, he raises important questions about the nature of evil and the factors that lead individuals down such a dark path.

Murderous Minds Australia serves as both an informative resource and a harrowing journey into the minds of serial killers who have left an indelible mark on Australian history. While exploring these chilling cases, we also reflect on the victims whose lives were tragically taken and the ripple effects that such atrocities have had on their communities.

Prepare yourself for a grim exploration of Australia's most terrifying criminals—those whose twisted desires have forever stained the otherwise idyllic image of this vast and diverse country. Whether you're a seasoned reader of true crime or newly captivated by this genre, this volume is a compelling and disturbing addition to Alan R. Warren's comprehensive series on the darkest facets of human nature.

ONE

David & Catherine Birnie

THE MOORHOUSE MURDERS

David and Catherine Birnie were an Australian couple from Perth who committed a series of murders in 1986, known as "The Moorhouse murders." Their murder spree was aptly named after their address at 3 Moorhouse Street in Willagee, which was a suburb of Perth. They murdered four women and attempted to murder a fifth. The Birnies' heinous acts shocked the nation and are remembered as some of the most notorious in Australian history.

Background

David Birnie was born on February 16, 1951. He was the oldest of five children in Wattle Grove, a semi-rural suburb of Perth. Even though they lived in the suburbs, the family was not known to be "normal," having regular meals together. Instead, the Birnie family was considered dysfunctional, given the rumors of alcoholism, promiscuity, and incest. In the early 1960s, the family moved to another suburb of Perth.

At fifteen, he left school to become an apprentice jockey for Eric Parnham at the Ascot Racecourse. During his time there, David developed a habit of exhibitionism and physically abused the horses. One night, wearing only stockings over his head, he broke into the room of an elderly lady where he was boarding and attempted to rape her.

As a teenager, David Birnie was frequently in and out of prison for various misdemeanors and felonies. As an adult, he became addicted to sex and pornography and was a paraphiliac.

In his early twenties, David met Catherine Harrison through mutual friends. They had a daughter named Tanya, who was ten years old at the time of his arrest for the murders. Tanya has since changed her surname and has never married or had children, stating, "I don't wanna spawn another David Birnie." During the time of the murders, in 1986, David Birnie was employed at a car wrecker's shop in Willagee.

Catherine Birnie, nee Catherine Margaret Harrison, was born on May 23, 1951. At the age of two, her mother, Doreen, died while giving birth to her brother, who also passed away two days later. Unable to care for Catherine, her father, Harold, sent her to live with her maternal grandparents. When Catherine was ten, a custody dispute resulted in Harold regaining sole custody.

Catherine first met David Birnie when she was twelve and began a romantic relationship with him two years later. Her father pleaded with her multiple times to leave David, as her involvement with him led to various legal troubles, ultimately resulting in her being sent to a youth prison. Later, a parole officer encouraged Catherine to work as a housekeeper for the McLaughlin family. On her 21st birthday, she married Donald McLaughlin, and they had seven children together over time.

Tragically, their firstborn son was struck and killed by a car during infancy.

But then, in 1985, Catherine left her family and resumed her relationship with David Birnie. They never legally married, but Catherine changed her surname to Birnie by deed poll—a legal document often used in some countries that is binding on a single person to express an intention or create an obligation.

Starting in October 1986, and over five weeks, David and Catherine Birnie abducted five women aged between fifteen and thirty-one. All but one of the victims were raped at the couple's residence (3 Moorhouse Street) and subsequently murdered. Their final victim, who managed to escape the day after her abduction and led the police back to the Birnie house, ended their crime spree.

Murders

Mary Neilson, a twenty-two-year-old psychology student at the University of Western Australia and part-time delicatessen worker, met David Birnie at the car wrecker's shop where he worked. David offered to sell her some cheap tires for her car and gave her his phone number. On October 6, 1986, Mary visited Birnie's residence at Moorhouse Street to look at the tires. Instead, she was gagged, chained to a bed, and raped by David while Catherine watched. She was then taken to Gleneagle, in Bedfordale, where she was raped again and strangled with a nylon cord. David also stabbed her, thinking it would speed up her decomposition. Catherine helped him bury her in a shallow grave. Mary Neilson would have received her psychology degree the following year.

Two weeks later, fifteen-year-old **Susannah Candy**, a high school student from Nedlands, was abducted while hitchhiking along the Stirling Highway in Claremont. Once inside the Birnies' car, Susannah was bound and held at knifepoint. They forced her to write letters to her family to assure them she was okay. Then, they took her to their home and subjected her to the same ordeal as Mary Neilson. After an initial failed attempt to strangle her with a nylon cord, they forced sleeping pills down her throat. Once the pills took effect, David wrapped the cord around her neck and told Catherine that she had to prove her love for him by killing her. Catherine complied, and

Susannah was buried close to Mary Neilson in Gleneagle.

When asked why she murdered Candy, Catherine claimed she believed she needed to murder Candy to see how strong she was inside. She also claimed that she didn't feel anything when she did it, just as she thought. Catherine believed that females only destroyed and hurt males in any way that they could. Therefore, she was willing to do anything to fulfill David's desires.

On November 1st, thirty-one-year-old **Noelene Patterson** ran out of gas on the Canning Highway while driving home from her job as a bar manager at the Nedlands Golf Club. Unfortunately, she was picked up by the Birnies and taken to their home, where David repeatedly raped her. Even though the initial plan was to murder Patterson that night, David kept her prisoner for three days. He later claimed this was due to an emotional attachment. Catherine became jealous of Noelene and eventually issued an ultimatum: David had to kill Noelene, or she would kill herself. David chose Catherine and forced Noelene to take an overdose of sleeping pills. He also strangled her after she fell asleep. They buried her body in Gleneagle as well, but Catherine insisted on burying her away from the other victims, reportedly taking great pleasure in throwing sand on her face.

———

On November 5th, the Birnies abducted twenty-one-year-old **Denise Brown** from a bus stop on Stirling Highway. Similar to their previous victims, Denise was taken at knifepoint and assaulted at their residence on Moorhouse Street. The following afternoon, the Birnies drove her to the Wanneroo pine plantation. In the secluded forest, David raped her in their car while waiting for it to get dark. After dragging Brown from the vehicle, David raped her again and then stabbed her in the neck. Believing she was dead, they began to bury her in a shallow grave. However, Brown sat up in the grave, prompting David to grab an axe and strike her twice in the head before burying her again.

———

On November 9th, seventeen-year-old **Kate Moir** was abducted at knifepoint after hitching a ride from the Birnies. David put a knife to her throat and forced her to call her mother, telling her that she was going to stay overnight at a friend's house because she had too much to drink. Kate asked the Birnies if they intended to kill or rape her, to which they responded that if she were good, she would only be raped. While they drank and laughed, she was instructed to dance for them. That night, she was handcuffed to David while they slept in bed.

The next day, David went to work, and Catherine, distracted by a drug deal, forgot to chain Kate to the bed. She broke a window lock and escaped, hitting her head on the concrete. After knocking on several neighbors' doors and getting no answer, she jumped a gate and was attacked by David's dog before finding refuge in a vacuum cleaner shop. There, she informed the owner that she had been raped. Bravely, she provided detailed information to the police, including the Birnies' address and telephone number.

Initially skeptical, the police were convinced by Constable Laura Handcock, who believed Kate's detailed account. She had read David's name on one of his prescription bottles, proving she was in the house. Police found a drawing she had made and Rocky's video cassette in the Birnies' VCR.

Both of the Birnies were arrested, and they gave conflicting information during their interviews. But eventually, David confessed and even revealed the burial sites of the victims.

It is believed that the Birnies could also be behind the disappearances of Cheryl Renwick in May and Barbara Western in June 1986. Going back even further to 1980, the police suspected that David could have been responsible for the disappearance of Lisa Marie Mott, but his first wife gave him an alibi by telling them that he was with her the whole day. This crime remains unsolved.

Trial & Imprisonment

At the trial, David Birnie pled guilty to four charges of murder and one charge each of abduction and rape. He claimed he pled guilty to the charges because he thought it was the least he could do for their family.

The Supreme Court of Western Australia sentenced both David and Catherine Birnet to four life sentences to be served in prison. Under the law at the time, both were required to serve twenty years before being eligible for parole.

David was placed in the maximum-security Fremantle Prison but was soon moved to solitary confinement to protect him from other prisoners. The prison renovated three of the death row cells to house him until the prison closed in 1991. Tourists on the *True Crime Tour* can still view the cell.

Catherine was imprisoned in Bandyup Women's Prison, where she works as a librarian and appears in a prison production of *Nunsense*. In 2007, her parole application was turned down by the then Attorney-General, who also said that she would never be released while he remained in office.

While incarcerated, the Birnies were not allowed to have personal contact but would write each other letters to communicate with each other. More than 2600 letters were sent between the two of them.

David was fifty-four when he was found dead

in his cell at Casuarina Prison on October 7, 2005, at 4:30 a.m. The medical report stated that he had hanged himself from the air vent in his cell by using a chord. Various factors led to his suicide, including a failure to provide him with his antidepressants, confiscation of his computer, and suspicion of sexually assaulting another prisoner. One former prison officer described him as a model prisoner who looked after injured animals. Prison authorities would not let Catherine go to his funeral.

Catherine's case was reviewed again in January 2010. On March 14, 2009, the new Attorney-General Christian Porter, after talking with the victims' families, decided that she would stay in jail for the rest of her life. The decision makes her the third Australian female prisoner— Katherine Knight and Patricia Byers being the first two—to be marked as never to be released. Catherine appealed this decision, but it was rejected in March 2010. Her fourth bid for parole was declined in 2016.

That same year, in 2016, Kate Moir began a campaign to end Western Australian laws that automatically put convicts up for parole every three years. She claimed that Catherine Birnie had never even applied for parole a few times they came up. In 2017, Catherine's youngest son, under the alias Peter, called for her execution, stating that his relation to her has resulted in him being assaulted on multiple occasions. He is a supporter of Kate Moir's campaign to end automatic parole.

TWO

Gregory Brazel

BLUEY

Gregory John "Bluey" Brazel, born on November 17, 1954, is a notorious Australian serial killer, arsonist, and armed robber, currently serving three life sentences consecutively. He was found guilty of the 1990 killings of Sharon Taylor and Roslyn Hayward, and then later, in 2000, he confessed to the 1982 murder of Mildred Hanmer. He was sentenced to twenty years in prison for the murders, which was reduced to seventeen years upon appeal.

Despite becoming eligible for parole in 2020, Brazel remains incarcerated at HM Prison Barwon as of 2024. He is often labeled one of Victoria's most manipulative and violent prisoners, and in 2000, his net worth was estimated at over 500,000 Australian dollars.

Background

Not much is known about Brazel's early life. We do know that he joined the Australian Army in 1974 at twenty years of age. In September of that year, he was assigned to the Australian Army Medical Training School in Healesville, Victoria. And in 1976, during a medical corps exercise, Brazel managed to take five of the privates hostage. Shots had to be fired before he would release them. After that, he received a dishonorable discharge.

Murders

Later, Brazel's criminal activities included murder. On May 28, 1990, while on early release from prison, he murdered sex worker **Sharon Taylor**, whose body was found in a shallow grave in Barongarook, Victoria. On September 13, 1990, he killed sex worker **Roslyn Hayward** in Sorrento. Her body was discovered on October 1, 1990. He was apprehended on September 26, 1990.

Brazel was remanded to HM Melbourne Assessment Prison. However, his deviant behavior continued even when he was behind bars. In November 1991, he took a staff member hostage after he found out that they intended to transfer him to HM Prison Pentridge.

In 1998, while in the high-security unit of HM Prison Barwon, Brazel was assaulted by fellow inmates. He sought and was granted access to documents, including a prison map and incident report, to sue the Victorian Government for failing to protect him.

In August 2000, Brazel confessed to the murder of **Mildred Teresa Hanmer**. He was seeking a plea deal to avoid a life sentence. Mildred was shot during an armed robbery at her store on September 20, 1982, and died from her injuries. Her case remained unsolved until Brazel confessed eighteen years later.

In May 2001, he was attacked with a broken bottle at the privately run Port Phillip Correctional Centre, and later, in an out-of-court settlement, he received A$12,000 in damages.

In October 2006, Brazel was caught collecting personal information such as names and home addresses of five senior prison staff members. It was discovered when jail authorities intercepted a letter written by Brazel that was being sent out of the maximum-security Barwon Prison. How he got the information is unknown, but what he had collected was accessible to the general public.

In 2022, Brazel accused prison officers of tampering with his mail and destroying his USB flash drive, resulting in the loss of 99% of his legal documents. His case against the State was scheduled for August 2023.

From March 1983 to August 2000, Brazel was convicted of thirty-seven offenses across fifteen court appearances. Since 1992, all offenses occurred while he was in prison, except for the 2005 conviction for a 1982 murder.

THREE

Eric Edgar Cooke

THE NIGHT CALLER

Eric Edgar Cooke was an Australian serial killer dubbed "The Night Caller," and later "The Nedlands Monster," who terrorized the city of Perth, Australia, from September 1958 to August 1963. During that time, Cooke committed at least twenty crimes, resulting in eight deaths. He was arrested and admitted to his crimes, including some that others had been wrongfully convicted.

The Supreme Court of Western Australia convicted Cooke of murder after a jury rejected his insanity defense. He was sentenced to death and hanged at Fremantle Prison, becoming the last person to be executed in Western Australia.

Background

Eric Edgar Cooke was born in Victoria Park, a suburb of Perth, Western Australia, on February 25, 1931. He was the eldest of three children and was born into a violent and unhappy family. His parents married, as was custom to do, when the couple got pregnant with him. Cooke was born with a cleft lip and palate, for which he underwent surgery at three months old and again at three and a half years old. These operations left him with a slight facial deformity and a speech impediment. Though slight, the disfigurement made him the target of bullying at school, resulting in his becoming emotionally unstable over time.

Growing up, his alcoholic father, Vivian

Cooke, frequently beat him, especially when he tried to protect his mother, Christine. To avoid the violence at home, his mother often slept in the staff room at her job in the Como Hotel, and Eric was frequently hospitalized for head injuries. He escaped his father's beatings on occasion by being placed in different orphanages or foster homes.

Cooke excelled in subjects requiring a good memory and manual dexterity. But he was caught stealing money from a teacher's purse and was expelled from Subiaco State School. He transferred schools but was abused and bullied by students at that school too.

Later, he was suspected of having brain damage due to his accident-proneness, and he was admitted to an asylum. His blackouts stopped after an operation in 1949.

At fourteen, Cooke quit school and went to work as a delivery boy for Central Provision Stores to support the family. He often gave his weekly wages to his mother, who struggled to support the family with her earnings from cooking and cleaning. Many of Cooke's jobs resulted in hospitalization due to his accident-proneness. When he was sixteen, he worked as a hammer boy in the blacksmith section at a workshop in

Midland Junction, where he always signed his lunch bag "Al Capone."

At age seventeen, rather than go home at night, Cooke spent his nights committing petty crimes, vandalism, and arson. He later served eighteen months in jail for burning down a church after being rejected in a choir audition. During his late teenage years, Cooke would sneak into houses to steal valuables, escalating to damaging clothing and furniture in acts of vengeance. He kept newspaper accounts of his crimes to impress acquaintances and gain friends.

On March 12, 1949, police arrested Cooke after they found evidence at his grandmother's house, where he was living. His fingerprints matched those found in a few open cases. On May 24, 1949, Cooke was convicted of two charges of theft, four charges of arson, and seven charges of breaking and entering and was sentenced to three years in prison.

As an adult, Cooke was a short, lightweight man with dark, wavy hair and a foul mouth. At twenty-one, he joined the regular Australian Army and was promoted to lance corporal during his training, where he learned to handle firearms. However, when his juvenile criminal record was discovered three months later, he was discharged.

On November 14, 1953, Cooke married nineteen-year-old waitress Sarah Lavin. They eventually had seven children, four boys and three girls.

During the 1950s and early 1960s, Cooke often stole cars at night, returning them without the owners even realizing. But in September 1955, he crashed one of the cars and was hospitalized. He was sentenced to two years of hard labor for unlawful use of a motor vehicle. Cooke was released from Fremantle Prison just before Christmas 1956. After his release, he wore gloves while committing crimes to avoid leaving fingerprints.

Murders

Cooke's killing spree was a series of hit-and-runs, stabbings, strangulations, and shootings that had no connections with each other. Brutally killing his victims in various ways and killing both men and women, there was no distinguishable MO. He either shot his victims with different rifles, stabbed them with knives or scissors, hit them with different cars, or beat them with an axe. Several of his victims were killed after waking up to find Cooke robbing their homes. Two were shot while they slept, and one was shot dead after answering the doorbell. After stabbing one victim, Cooke drank lemonade from the refrigerator while sitting on the veranda. One victim was strangled with a bedside lamp cord, and after they were dead, Cooke raped the body, disrobed it, and dragged it to a neighbor's lawn. He then sexually penetrated it with an empty whisky bottle, which he left cradled in the victim's arms.

Cooke's murder victims were **Jillian McPherson Brewer**, **Pnena Berkman**, **John Lindsay Sturkey**, **George Ormond Walmsley**, **Rosemary Anderson**, **Constance Lucy Madrill**, **Shirley Martha McLeod**, and **Brian Vincent Weir.** Another victim died three years after being shot by Cooke.

Due to the varying methods and opportunistic nature of his crimes, it was not initially thought that one individual committed all of them. The murders of Jillian Brewer and Rosemary Anderson were blamed on other men who were wrongfully convicted.

The police investigation involved fingerprinting more than 30,000 males over the age of twelve and locating and test-firing more than 60,000 .22 rifles. In August 1963, a gun hidden in a bush on Rookwood Street, Mount

Pleasant, was found, and ballistic tests proved it had been used in the McLeod murder. Police set up a surveillance operation, and Cooke was arrested when he tried to collect the weapon just after midnight on September 1st.

Initially denying involvement in the McLeod murder, Cooke confessed after a detective confronted him, emphasizing the impact on his family and his undoubted execution if he kept denying his guilt. Eventually, he admitted to eight murders and fourteen attempted murders, along with more than 250 burglaries.

Trial & Execution

On November 25, 1963, Cooke stood trial for the murder of John Lindsay Sturkey, where he pled not guilty on the grounds of insanity. His lawyers claimed he had schizophrenia, but the Court believed the Director of the State Mental Health Services, who testified that Cooke was sane. The State did not allow independent psychiatric specialists to examine Cooke. After a three-day trial, it took a jury of eight men and four women just over an hour to reach their verdict. He was convicted of murder and was sentenced to death. Despite having grounds to appeal, Cooke ordered his lawyers not to, claiming he deserved to pay for his actions.

Cooke was hanged at 8 a.m. on October 26, 1964, in Fremantle Prison, eleven months after being sentenced. Ten minutes before his execution, he swore on the Bible that he had killed Jillian Brewer and Rosemary Anderson, whose murders had been attributed to and resulted in the wrongful conviction of other men.

Cooke was the last convicted prisoner to be hanged in Western Australia and was buried above the body of child killer Martha Rendell, who was the last woman to be hanged in Fremantle Prison in Fremantle Cemetery in 1909.

Wrongful Convictions

Two other men were convicted of murders Cooke had committed. In December 1961, Darryl Beamish, a deaf-mute, was convicted of the murder of Jillian Brewer. She was stabbed to death with scissors and hit on the head with an axe in 1959. Beamish was initially sentenced to death, but after an appeal, the sentence was commuted to life imprisonment. When Cooke confessed to Brewer's murder before his execution in 1964, the Court did not believe his evidence.

They dismissed Cooke's confession and called him a "villainous unscrupulous liar." Beamish served fifteen years before his conviction was quashed in 2005, following a long campaign supported by *Post Newspapers'* owner Bret Christian.

A second man, John Button, was wrongfully convicted of murdering his girlfriend, Rosemary Anderson, in 1963. Anderson died in the Perth Hospital on February 10, 1963. She had spent the day before with Button, celebrating his nineteenth birthday. They had a minor argument, and she decided to walk home. Button followed her in his car, trying to persuade her to accept a ride. But she refused. He pulled over for a cigarette to give her time to cool down. When he looked for her again, he found her injured on the roadside. He took her to a doctor, but she died in hospital the next day. Button was convicted of manslaughter after intense police questioning led to a confession. He was sentenced to ten years in prison. Despite Cooke's confession to the crime in 1964, Button's appeals were dismissed. He ended up serving five and a half years.

Over the decades, Button and his supporters refused to give up. They continued to try to prove his innocence. In 1998, a simulated reenactment of the incident and further evidence eventually led to Button's acquittal in 2002.

In 2002, the Appeals Court quashed John Button's conviction, and he was granted an A$460,000 ex gratia payment for the wrongful conviction. Darryl Beamish was acquitted in 2005. On June 2, 2011, the Western Australian government also awarded him an A$425,000 ex gratia payment.

FOUR

Paul Denyer

THE FRANSTON SERIAL KILLER

P aul Denyer, briefly known as Paula while in prison, is an Australian serial killer serving three consecutive life sentences with a minimum of thirty years for the murders of three women in Melbourne in 1993. His crimes earned him the moniker "The Frankston Serial

Killer" as they occurred in neighboring suburbs of Frankston.

During his imprisonment, around the age of thirty, Denyer began identifying as a transgender woman. However, prison authorities refused to allow him to dress like a woman, use make-up, have a sex reassignment surgery, or legally change his name. According to John Silvester in the 2022 Stan documentary *No Mercy, No Remorse*, Denyer has since reverted to identifying as Paul.

In 2023, Denyer became eligible for parole and applied for release, but the Adult Parole Board of Victoria denied his application.

Background

Paul Charles Denyer was born on April 14, 1972, in Campbelltown, New South Wales, a suburb of Sydney. He was the child of Anthony and Maureen Denyer, who started dating and married in the early 1960s in London, England, before moving to Australia in 1965. In 1981, the family moved to Victoria for the father's work opportunities.

As a youth, Paul Denyer had difficulty fitting in among his peers in his new school. His inability to fit in led to problems with his studies and personal life. Later, his self-confidence worsened by his significant weight gain during his teen years. At age ten, he slashed the throat of his sister's toy and cut the throat of the family cat before hanging it in a tree. Just before turning thirteen, he was charged with stealing a car. At age fifteen, he was arrested for assaulting a fellow student.

After leaving school, he had problems holding down jobs. He was fired seven times and failed the physical when trying to enter the Victoria Police Academy. In February 1993, Denyer started working at a boatbuilding firm, but a short time later, coworkers observed him making knives while at work. Denyer was let go a few months after failing to complete several assigned tasks.

In the months leading up to the murders, Denyer began stalking and attacking women in and around the Melbourne suburb of Frankston. This behavior lasted for about five months. Denyer's first known incident happened in February 1993, when Donna Vanes' unit on Claude Street in Seaford was broken into.

Following an anonymous threatening call, Donna became fearful of being alone and asked her boyfriend to take her and their newborn baby with him while he delivered pizzas. After being out for about an hour, they returned to find blood on the floor and one of their cats dead. When police arrived, they found the dead cat had also been dissected, someone had put a pornographic image on its body, and the words "Donna, you're dead" were written in the cat's blood above the stove.

Police also found Donna's two kittens, with their throats cut, floating dead in the bathtub. In their bedroom, shaving cream had been sprayed over a mirror, and more slashed pornographic pictures were placed over a wardrobe and some other furniture. One of the slashed pornographic images had been placed inside the crib of her baby.

For her safety, Donna moved in with her sister, who happened to live next to Paul Denyer. Her sister's neighbor had recently been the victim of a similar break-in and vandalism.

After Denyer's arrest, he confessed to the break-in, vandalism, and killing Donna Vanes' cats. He admitted to police that had she been home, he would have murdered her.

Murders

The first known murder victim of Paul Denyer was eighteen-year-old **Elizabeth Stevens**. She had moved to Melbourne from Tasmania in January 1993 to study at TAFE Frankston, aspiring to join the armed forces. On the evening of Friday, June 11, 1993, at approximately 7:00 p.m., Elizabeth got off a bus on Cranbourne Road, the closest stop to her aunt and uncle's house, where she was staying. She had been living with them for six months.

As Elizabeth turned onto Paterson Avenue, she was grabbed from behind and threatened with what appeared to be a gun. She screamed, but her screams went unheard due to heavy rain and wind. She was forced to walk down Paterson Avenue, with her assailant holding her hand to avoid drawing suspicion. Several witnesses saw them walking together and assumed they were a couple.

The pair arrived at Lloyd Park Reserve, where Elizabeth was sexually propositioned but then reassured that he posed no sexual threat. Denyer then strangled, stabbed, and cut her throat. Her attacker stomped on her face, breaking several facial bones, and then dragged her a short distance to a ditch. She had been stabbed and slashed across the torso after her death.

Elizabeth had left a note for her relatives that morning, stating she would be studying at the TAFE or city library and home by 8:00 p.m. When she did not return home, her relatives thought she might be running late. At 10:30 p.m., her uncle began driving around the area searching for her. Police were notified soon after and became concerned after seeing the note she had written. Her body was discovered around 5:00 p.m. the following day by a man collecting pine branches. Elizabeth was killed only 250 meters from her home.

The post-mortem examination revealed hemorrhages, indicating strangulation. Cuts and abrasions to the face were also observed. The forensic pathologist concluded that the cause of death was aspiration of blood and bleeding from stab wounds to the neck.

They conducted an extensive search of the area where Elizabeth's body was found, along with the surrounding streets. A bag containing books and documents in her name and the blade of a knife was discovered. Police interviewed every nearby resident and rode the local bus to see if any passengers recognized her. Despite these efforts, investigators never found any solid leads on her movements or clues that would solve her murder.

A month after the murder of Elizabeth Stevens, forty-one-year-old **Rosza Toth** left the train station and headed north along the Railway Parade on her way home on Thursday, July 8, 1993. Walking around 5:50 p.m., she noticed a man loitering near the toilet. She was attacked shortly after passing him. Rosza was dragged towards the unlit park, with her attacker holding a gun to her head. However, quickly realizing it was fake, Rosza decided to fight back. She broke away from his grip, managed to break free, and returned to the main road. She saw a car driving towards her and was able to flag it down. The driver took her to her house, where she called police.

On the same night, twenty-two-year-old **Deborah Fream**, who lived near Kananook Station in Seaford, was abducted in her car in the early evening. Deborah ran out to get milk around 7:00 p.m., leaving her twelve-day-old son with a male friend at home. After she had not returned home by 8:00 p.m., her friend started to call around, trying to find her. Her boyfriend hadn't heard from her, so he checked their local hospital to see if she was involved in an accident or something, but she wasn't there. The friend and her boyfriend drove around to locate her. When they couldn't, they reported her missing at Frankston Police Station.

On the afternoon of Monday, July 12th, Deborah's partially covered body was discovered by a farmer on Taylors Road in Carrum Downs. Like Elizabeth Stevens, she had been strangled with a cord, savagely slashed, and her throat cut.

Denyer's third and final victim, seventeen-year-old student **Natalie Russell**, was attacked on Friday, July 30, 1993, while walking home from John Paul College. At the time, there was a lot of news about the recent murders, which heightened public fear and warnings from her school. Natalie always rode her bike to school with her brother, but that day, she was driven by her mother as a precaution.

She left school early by herself and took her usual route home through a fenced walkway between two golf courses on Skye Road.

The Frankston Police Station received a report about Natalie not coming home from school around eight that evening. Police began to search the area and soon found her dead body, which had been dragged down the walkway and through a large hole in a wire fence into the field. Like the other victims, she had been strangled and her throat cut. During the attack, she had put up a considerable fight, leaving DNA evidence that assisted investigators.

Investigation

Police involvement in Paul Denyer's case began after the incidents at his block of units and Donna Vanes' unit in February 1993. The murder of Elizabeth Stevens triggered a significant investigation, as did the disappearance of Deborah Fream. The investigation was so thorough that it even led to a search that included scuba divers examining Kananook Creek.

No external forensic evidence was found at Elizabeth Stevens' murder scene, and no witnesses came forward. In the case of Deborah Fream, poor weather conditions prevented the collection of forensic evidence at the scene. However, it was evident that she had fought her attacker. Witnesses later reported seeing her car, a gray Nissan Pulsar, driving erratically and flashing its high-beam lights. Police found her unlocked car the next day on Madden Street, with traces of her blood inside, a new dent in the front, and the driver's seat pushed back. Denyer later explained that he had found her car unlocked at a milk bar, climbed into the back seat, and threatened her with a replica gun shortly after she drove away.

Following her attack, Rosza Toth described her assailant as a man aged between eighteen and twenty years old, approximately 180 cm tall (5' 9"), with a round face and blue eyes. From her description, the police created a profile of the suspect: male, likely unemployed or in a menial job, living locally and alone, aged eighteen to twenty-four, and average-looking.

In the lead-up to the murder of Natalie Russell, two hundred investigators were visiting 4,700 homes in the area around Madden Street, Frankston, as part of "Operation Pulsar," named after Deborah Fream's vehicle. The door-to-door inquiry was the largest ever conducted by Victoria Police at the time.

As media scrutiny and community concern grew, detectives began to connect other incidents as well, suspecting links in the case of Sarah MacDiarmid, who went missing in 1990, and Michelle Brown's murder in 1992.

Natalie Russell's attack provided the breakthrough police needed. A postal worker noticed a man inside his rusted yellow Toyota Corona without license plates parked near Nat's Track on Skye Road. He was using binoculars and acting suspiciously. As the postal worker stopped at a house to call the police, she saw Natalie approach the track alone. Natalie was watched by the suspicious man, who then ran up the track. Police responded, recorded the registration label number, and knocked on a few nearby houses before leaving for another call.

On the walkway Natalie took on her way home from school, detectives found three holes cut in the fence. The tool used had blood traces and skin and hair traces that did not belong to the victim.

Arrest

Registration of the car was traced to Paul Charles Denyer. Detectives visited his unit at 186

Frankston-Dandenong Road, Seaford, which he shared with his girlfriend. It was next door to Donna Vanes' sister. Denyer admitted to being in the area of the Fream and Russell murders at the time. So, he was taken to Frankston Police Station for further questioning.

Denyer's videoed interview began at 9:20 p.m. He could not adequately explain the cuts and scratches the officers noticed on him. He admitted to being in the area of the Stevens attack, and he agreed to have his DNA collected.

Early on August 1st, suspecting that the police had DNA evidence, he confessed to the murders, the Toth assault, and the slasher break-ins. Denyer told detectives he had been stalking women in the Frankston area "for years" and that his motivation for the crimes stemmed from a desire to kill since the age of fourteen and a general hatred of girls and women.

Paul Denyer was charged with three counts of murder and one count of abduction, to which he later pleaded guilty without contest. He was examined by a court psychiatrist who said that he had a total lack of any emotions about any of the crimes, as well as a single-minded desire to kill, learned by the unusual randomness by which he chose his victims. Denyer also admitted during his examination that the 1987 film *The Stepfather* influenced him. He was diagnosed as having a sadistic personality disorder but not legal insanity.

Trial & Imprisonment

The trial lasted only four days, and on December 20, 1993, Denyer was sentenced to three consecutive terms of life with no chance of parole. On December 31st, he appealed. In July 1994, he was granted a non-parole period of thirty years. He was eligible for parole in 2023 and applied for it but was denied.

Initially, Denyer was sent to the Melbourne Assessment Prison, where he befriended Robert Lowe, then to HM Prison Barwon, and currently, he is at Port Phillip Prison.

Paul Denyer wrote a series of letters in 2003 and 2004 to another inmate called "The Paul Denyer Letters." In the first letter, dated November 29, 2003, he began identifying as a woman. He claimed that his feelings of gender dysphoria made him seek revenge against women by murdering them. In subsequent letters, he described these feelings in more detail. He claimed that he committed his crimes only because he never felt comfortable living as a man. He began to dress in women's clothing and started using make-up in prison, which was against prison rules. He started referring to himself as "Paula." He requested to have a sex change operation, but prison authorities turned it down. He has since reverted to being called Paul.

FIVE

Peter Dupas

Peter Dupas is an Australian serial killer serving three life sentences without parole. His criminal history was marked by brutal sexual and violent offenses against women that span over three decades. Each time when he was released from prison, he went on to commit even more crimes against women that were more and more brutal each time. He is notorious for his gruesome criminal signature of removing his female victims' breasts.

Dupas was convicted of three murders and remains a suspect in at least three other murders that occurred in the Melbourne area during the 1980s and 1990s.

Background

Peter Norris Dupas was born in Sydney, New South Wales, on July 6, 1953. He was the youngest of three children born to an average family that relocated to Melbourne, Victoria, when he was a toddler. Dupas felt like an only child growing up because his siblings were so much older than he was. After finishing grade ten, he quit school but later earned a high school diploma.

Crimes against Women

On October 3, 1968, Dupas, fifteen years old at the time, approached his next-door neighbor, asking to borrow a knife to peel some vegetables. He used it to stab the woman in the face, neck, and hand as she fought off his attack. He was later apprehended. He told the police that he could not control himself and did not understand why he attacked her. After receiving an eighteen-month probation sentence, he was sent to the Larundel Psychiatric Hospital for evaluation. He was released after only two weeks and treated as an outpatient.

A year later, in 1969, the morgue at the Austin Hospital was broken into, and the bodies of two older women were mutilated with a pathologist's knife. One body had a peculiar wound on the thigh. Later, the police suspected Dupas was involved in the break-in, as the scars matched those inflicted on his murder victim, Nicole Patterson.

On July 25, 1974, Dupas was sentenced to nine years in prison for an assault on a woman in her home. He broke into her house, threatened her with a knife, tied her up with a cord, and raped her, even threatening to harm her baby when she resisted. The sentencing judge described the crime as "one of the worst rapes that could be imagined." After his sentencing, prison psychiatrist Dr. Allen Bartholomew noted that Dupas denied any criminal action.

Only two months after his release from prison,

in 1979, Dupas committed a series of assaults, molesting women in four separate attacks over ten days. He received a five-year prison sentence for three convictions of assault with the intent of sexual assault and assault with intent to rob. After a trial in late February 1980, a psychological report on Dupas noted that he remained "extremely disturbed and a dangerous man."

One month after Dupas was released in 1985, he sexually assaulted a twenty-one-year-old woman on a beach at Blairgowrie, Victoria. He followed her after getting out of his car, attacked her, and held her at knifepoint before raping her. After he was arrested, he told police that he didn't think he would do it again after being released that last time and that he was sorry he did it. He claimed he was normal and just trying to live an everyday life. This time, Dupas was sentenced to twelve years in prison but was released in 1992 after only serving seven years.

Less than two years after his release, in January 1994, Dupas was arrested and charged with another violent crime against women. He was wearing a hood that covered most of his face and was armed with a knife, masking tape, and handcuffs. He followed a woman who was picnicking with her friends. When she went into the washroom alone, he followed her and held her at knifepoint. Fortunately, her friends were watching out for her, and when she didn't return, they went to check on her. They chased him off. As he tried to drive away, he crashed his car and was apprehended. On August 18, 1994, he pleaded guilty to false imprisonment and was sentenced to three years and nine months in prison. In September 1996, Dupas was rereleased from jail and moved to the suburbs of Melbourne.

Murders

Twenty-eight-year-old **Nicole Patterson** was a youth counselor working for the Ardoch Youth Foundation, an organization dedicated to helping young drug users. Nicole aspired to run a private practice and used her home in Northcote as her office. To attract more clients, she placed several classified ads in the local Northcote Leader newspaper.

On April 19, 1999, the day of Nicole's murder, two neighbors reported hearing a young woman's screams that sounded like they were coming from her home around nine in the morning. Later that afternoon, her boyfriend grew suspicious when he could not reach her.

A friend of Nicole's discovered her body in the front room of her Harper Street residence. The friend had come for a dinner engagement and entered the house upon hearing music from a radio and finding the front door unlocked. Inside, she found Nicole's body severely mutilated.

Nicole had died from twenty-seven stab wounds to her chest and back. She was discovered naked from the waist down, with her skirt in a nearby bedroom and her underwear around her ankles. Small pieces of yellow PVC tape were found attached to her body, and her breasts had been removed with a sharp knife. Her handbag and driver's license were also missing. The murder weapon and her breasts were never recovered.

Nicole's diary revealed that she had scheduled a 9 a.m. appointment with a new client named "Malcolm." A mobile phone number was also noted there. The number was traced to an Indian student at La Trobe University named "Harry." Police discovered that Peter Dupas had approached Harry with an offer of labor work.

Telephone records showed that Dupas had made three prior calls to Nicole to arrange a counseling session. He claimed he had depression and a gambling addiction. The first call originated from a public telephone booth approximately six weeks before her murder. Over the following weeks, Dupas continued calling Nicole to assess any vulnerabilities. He later claimed he canceled his appointment after she suggested his issues could be managed independently.

On April 22, 1999, Dupas was found at the Excelsior Hotel in Thomastown and brought in for questioning. Police observed scratches on Dupas' face and hand, indicating a recent struggle. He initially claimed the scratches were from working in his backyard shed, and a piece of wood hit him while using a lathe. However, he did not own a lathe. He later revised his story, stating the injuries occurred while walking by a protruding piece of wood in the shed.

A search of Dupas' home uncovered blood-stained clothing, PVC tape matching what was found at the crime scene, a ski mask, newspaper clippings about Nicole's murder, and a paper containing her psychotherapy service advertisement.

Dupas was arrested and charged with Nicole's murder. Later, after the trial, the jury deliberated for less than three hours, finding Peter Dupas guilty of Nicole's murder. On August 22, 2000, Judge Frank Vincent sentenced Dupas to life imprisonment without the possibility of parole.

He appealed the conviction in August 2001, but it was dismissed.

While Dupas was already serving a life sentence without parole for the murder of Nicole Patterson, he was arrested for another murder that occurred in 1997. **Margaret Josephine Maher**, a forty-year-old sex worker, was last seen alive at the Safeway Supermarket in Broadmeadows at 12:20 a.m. on October 4, 1997. While a man and his wife were out collecting aluminum in Somerton, they found Margaret's body under a cardboard box containing computer parts. Nearby, police found a black woolen glove containing DNA that matched Peter Dupas'. During this time, Dupas was out of prison for over a year serving time for rape offenses and was no longer on probation.

The Medical Examiner found that Margaret had been stabbed in her left wrist and had a bruise above her right eyebrow from being hit with a cinderblock. She had cuts on her right arm and bruises on her neck. Her left breast had been removed and then put into her mouth.

Once the police obtained a DNA sample from

Dupas during Nicole Patterson's investigation, he was linked to Margaret's 1997 murder as well.

During a three-week trial, the jury was presented with evidence that the removal of the breasts of Nicole Patterson and Margaret Maher was so "strikingly similar" that it served as a signature or trademark stamp of one killer. Such a unique act identified Peter Dupas as the same killer of both women. The jury took less than a day to convict him of his second murder. Upon hearing the guilty verdict, Dupas claimed, "It's a kangaroo court," before being led away to begin his sentence.

Kylie Nicholas, Nicole Patterson's sister, described Dupas as a psychopath, predator, and repulsive person outside of the courthouse after he was sentenced. "We pray that this man is held accountable for everything he has done." Ian Joblin, a psychologist, wrote a report on Dupas claiming that he attacked these women "to fulfill his fantasies of conquest and control." Yet each of his attacks left him unsatisfied and looking for another victim. The unfulfilled feeling led to Dupas continuing his attacks on women in the hopes that he would one day be satisfied.

On August 16, 2004, Dupas was convicted of murdering Margaret Maher and sentenced to a second term of life imprisonment. During sentencing, Judge Kaye remarked that he would have sentenced Dupas to a life term for his next crime, even if it had not been a murder, due to his being a severe violent habitual offender with no signs of rehabilitation. On July 25, 2005, the Supreme Court of Victoria Court of Appeal dismissed Dupas' appeal for this murder.

Also, in 1997, twenty-six-year-old **Mersina Halvagis** was visiting her grandmother's grave at Fawkner Cemetery in Fawkner, Melbourne, when she went missing. When she failed to meet her fiancé as planned on November 1, 1997, it worried him, so he went to look for her. He found her body at 4:35 a.m. on November 5th in an empty plot three graves away from her grandmother's. Mersina's sweater and blouse had been pulled up over her head. She had suffered massive injuries, including eighty-seven stab wounds around her knees, neck, and, most extensively, on her breasts.

Dupas had been living near the Fawkner Cemetery, and despite extensive investigation, her murder remained unsolved for years. The

Victorian state government and police offered a one million dollar reward for information that led to the arrest of the person responsible for her murder.

Several witnesses linked Dupas to the Fawkner Cemetery on the day of Mersina's murder, including nine who said that they saw him there the same day. One witness also told police that she saw him only minutes before the attack occurred in the cemetery.

Since Dupas was already in prison when they connected him to Mersina's murder, a court order was required to transport him from HM Prison Barwon to the St Kilda Road Police Headquarters in Melbourne on September 2, 2006, for questioning. Dupas claimed that he went to that cemetery because his grandfather was buried there, only 128 meters from where Mersina's body was discovered. He also claimed that he was in the area because he regularly went to a bar in the hotel just across the street from the cemetery.

Senior Detective Scarlett testified that Dupas' car, owned at the time of the murder, was sold shortly after, and it was later crushed for scrap metal, preventing forensic examination. Forensic pathologist Professor David Ransom, who compared the wounds suffered by Mersina to those of Nicole and Margaret, concluded there was insufficient evidence to suggest the wounds were inflicted using the same knife or by the same person.

Dupas' lawyer, David Drake, argued that the only evidence linking Dupas to Mersina's murder was his proximity to the cemetery and his reputation based on prior similar offenses. He asserted that the police relied on the assumption that Dupas had a propensity to attack women with knives, thus linking him to the crime.

On September 11, 2006, Dupas was formally charged with Mersina's murder following a revelation by disgraced Melbourne lawyer Andrew Fraser. Fraser disclosed that Dupas had confessed to the killing while they were gardening at Port Phillip Prison in 2002. Fraser recounted an incident where he found a homemade knife concealed among the weeds in the prison garden and called Dupas to inspect it. According to Fraser, they often found drugs or weapons that Dupas had hidden in the garden. He remembers once when Dupas made a homemade knife, and he would touch it sensually. He called the knife "Mersina" when he showed it off.

Following his agreement to testify against Dupas, Fraser was released from prison on

September 11, 2006, two months before he was supposed to be released for his drug trafficking conviction. The Victorian government also declared that Fraser was allowed to apply to receive the one million dollar cash reward that had been offered for information leading to the arrest of Mersina's murderer.

Prosecutors withdrew the murder charge against Dupas in the Melbourne Magistrates' Court, requesting that the case be sent directly to trial, bypassing the committal hearing process. Dupas appeared through video camera to the Supreme Court of Victoria on September 26, 2006, charged with the murder of Mersina Halvagis, and entered a plea of not guilty. Dupas' barrister argued that his client was unfairly treated by skipping the usual committal hearing process. The Supreme Court said they would provide their ruling on whether Dupas would face a committal hearing in November of that year.

Dupas appeared before Justice John Coldrey at the Supreme Court of Victoria on November 14, 2006, to request the opportunity to cross-examine witness Andrew Fraser before a criminal trial.

The trial for the murder of Mersina Halvagis was supposed to begin in early July 2007. However, on July 9, 2007, Prosecutor Colin

Hillman SC informed Justice Philip Cummins that there had been a failure to comply with the Jury Act, as potential jurors were not advised of the possible trial duration. The jury was discharged on this legal technicality, delaying the trial.

The trial ran for twenty-two days once it finally got started. Prosecution witness Andrew Fraser described to the jury how Dupas described his attack on Mersina Halvagis. By then, Fraser had already submitted the $1 million reward claim.

On August 9, 2007, Dupas was found guilty of the murder of Mersina Halvagis. Three days later, he was sentenced to his third life sentence with no chance of parole. The sentencing was on live television, becoming the first televised sentencing in Australia since the 1995 sentencing of child killer Nathan John Avent.

An appeal was submitted on September 10, 2007, arguing that the guilty verdict for the Halvagis murder trial was unsafe and unsatisfactory. On September 17, 2009, his appeal was upheld by a two-to-one majority in Victoria's Court of Appeal, which ruled that the judge had given inadequate directions.

A new trial began on October 26, 2010, in the Victorian Supreme Court, and on November 19,

2010, Dupas was again convicted of the murder after three-and-a-half days of jury deliberations. He was later sentenced to life in prison without the possibility of parole.

Other Possible Victims

Forty-seven-year-old **Helen McMahon** was found beaten to death, naked, covered with a beach towel, on a Rye beach on February 13, 1985. She was sunbathing topless. The murder occurred at a location near where a twenty-one-year-old woman had been raped earlier. The same rape that Dupas was convicted of and served a prison term for in 1985. At the time of Helen's murder, police first believed that Dupas was in prison but later learned that he had been released two weeks prior and was living in the Rye area when she was killed. Helen's murder is still officially unsolved, but police still consider Dupas the prime suspect.

Dupas is also a suspect in the murder of thirty-one-year-old **Renita Brunton**, who was killed on November 5, 1993. She was found stabbed over one hundred times in the clothing store kitchen that she owned in Sunbury, Victoria.

Ninety-five-year-old **Kathleen Downes** was

living at the Brunswick Lodge nursing home in Brunswick when she was found stabbed to death in her house on the morning of December 31, 1997. It was one month after the murder of Mersina Halvagis. Police investigations revealed that Dupas had telephoned the nursing home the night before Downes was murdered. In February 2018, he was officially charged with her murder.

Marriage in Prison

While Dupas was serving time in Melbourne's Pentridge Prison, he formed a relationship with Grace McConnell, a mental health nurse who was sixteen years older than him. They were married in Castlemaine Gaol in 1987 but divorced during the mid-1990s.

SIX

William MacDonald

THE (SYDNEY) MUTILATOR

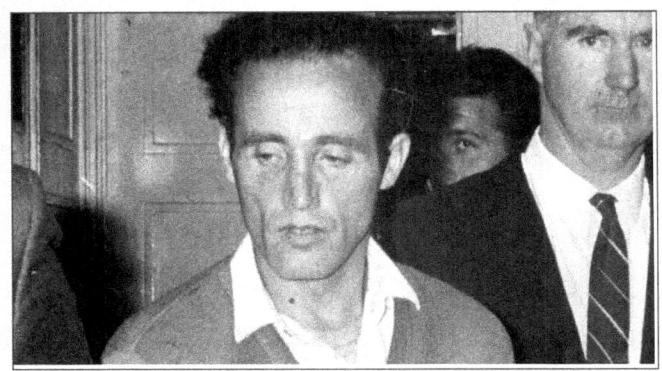

William MacDonald was an English serial killer responsible for the murders of five people in Australia between 1961 and 1962. He terrorized Sydney with a string of gruesome murders before being apprehended in 1963. His modus operandi was to select male victims at random, lure them into a dark place, violently punch and stab them with a knife dozens of times about the upper body, and finally sever their genitals. The media dubbed him "The Mutilator" due to his gruesome style of murdering victims.

Background

William MacDonald was born Allen Ginsberg on June 17, 1924, in Liverpool, England. Not much is known about his early life, but in 1943, at nineteen years old, he enlisted in the Army and transferred to the Lancashire Fusiliers. He was raped one night by a corporal while in an air-raid shelter. It was an experience that traumatized him and haunted him for the rest of his life. After being discharged from the Army in 1947, he was diagnosed with schizophrenia and committed to a mental asylum for several months, where he underwent daily electroshock therapy.

In 1949, he changed his name from Allen Ginsberg to William MacDonald and emigrated from England to Canada. He got into some trouble with the law there, and in 1955, he moved to Australia. Shortly after he arrived in Adelaide, he was charged with touching the penis of an undercover police detective in a public washroom. The result was being placed on a two-year good behavior bond.

MacDonald lived in Ballarat for a while but then moved to Sydney in 1961, where he worked as a construction worker and found accommodation in East Sydney. He became well known in the parks and public toilets, which were clandestine meeting places for homosexual men— "clandestine" because of the criminalization of same-sex sexual activity at the time.

Murders

The murders began in Brisbane in May 1961. MacDonald met sixty-three-year-old **Amos Hugh Hurst** outside the Roma Street Railway Station. After a long drinking session at a local pub, they returned to Amos' apartment and continued drinking. When Amos became heavily intoxicated, MacDonald began to strangle him. Amos, too drunk to know what was happening to him, eventually started bleeding from his mouth. When MacDonald realized that Amos was bleeding all over his hands, he began to punch him in the face until he died. He placed Amos on the bed, removed his trousers and shoes, and tucked the sheets around him before turning off the lights and leaving the apartment. The papers reported it as an accidental death.

MacDonald moved to Sydney, and calling himself Alan Edward Brennan, he got a job at the post office.

On June 4, 1961, police were called to the Sydney Domain Baths, where they found the naked corpse of forty-one-year-old **Alfred Reginald Greenfield**, who had been savagely stabbed over thirty times, with his genitals wholly severed. Later, it was learned from witnesses that Alfred was relaxing at Green Park when he met MacDonald. The two had a couple of drinks before going to the bathhouse. After Alfred fell asleep a few hours later, Macdonald stabbed him to death. He then pulled Alfred's pants off, cut off his genitals, and placed them into a plastic bag that he had brought with him so that he could later take them to the Sydney Harbor, where he planned to throw them in the water.

In November of that year, thirty-seven-year-old **Ernest William Cobbin** was found stabbed and mutilated in a public toilet at Moore Park. MacDonald met Ernest while walking down South Dowling Street and lured him to Moore Park, where they drank beer in a public toilet. Before the attack, MacDonald put on a plastic raincoat. He then struck Ernest in the neck with a knife, severing his jugular vein. Ernest tried to defend himself, but MacDonald continued stabbing him multiple times. MacDonald severed Ernest's genitals, placed them in a plastic bag with his knife, and left the scene.

On March 31, 1962, MacDonald struck again, and **Frank Gladstone McLean** was found mortally wounded in Darlinghurst, New South Wales. MacDonald had bought a knife that day and followed Frank after leaving the Oxford Hotel. He suggested they have a drink together in Bourke Lane, where MacDonald stabbed Frank in the throat. Frank, too intoxicated to fight back effectively, was stabbed multiple times. The attack was interrupted by a young family, causing MacDonald to hide. After the family left,

MacDonald returned to finish the job. He dragged Frank further into the lane and stabbed him again. He then severed Frank's genitals and put them in a plastic bag.

After being dismissed from his job at the local post office, MacDonald went into business for himself, purchasing a mixed business store in Concord, again under the name Alan Edward Brennan.

On June 6, 1962, MacDonald met thirty-seven-year-old **Patrick Joseph Hackett** at a wine saloon on Pitt Street, Sydney. They went back to MacDonald's new residence and continued drinking until Patrick fell asleep. MacDonald then stabbed him in the neck with a boning knife. Patrick woke and tried to defend himself, but MacDonald continued the attack, eventually killing him. Unable to sever Patrick's genitals with the blunted knife, MacDonald fell asleep exhausted.

MacDonald awoke the following day covered in blood, cleaned himself, and went to a hospital to have his injured hand stitched. He dragged Patrick's body underneath his shop and fled to

Brisbane, believing the police would soon find the body.

Three weeks later, the neighbors detected a putrid smell coming from MacDonald's shop and called the health department, who contacted the police. It wasn't until November 20, 1962, when police discovered the rotting corpse. It was too decomposed to be identified immediately, but the autopsy determined it was a male in their forties. So they assumed it was the missing shop owner, Alan Brennan (MacDonald's alias). The police had not yet connected this case to the previous Mutilator killings, as they believed the killer operated in Sydney's inner eastern suburbs, far from Concord.

A notice of Alan Brennan's death was published in a newspaper obituary column, which his former workmates read at the local post office. They attended a small memorial service conducted by a local funeral director. Meanwhile, MacDonald was hiding out in Brisbane and then New Zealand, believing the police were looking for him. Feeling the need to kill again, he returned to Sydney.

Back in Sydney, MacDonald ran into a former workmate, John McCarthy, who expressed shock, saying, "I believed you had died." MacDonald replied, "Leave me alone," and ran away as fast as possible. He eventually went to Melbourne. John McCarthy reported the encounter to the police, but they initially did not believe him. They accused him of being drunk or crazy. Frustrated, McCarthy went to the *Daily Mirror* newspaper and spoke to crime reporter Joe Morris, who found the story credible and published it under the headline "Case of the Walking Corpse."

Publication of the article forced the police to exhume the body found in the shop, revealing it to belong to Patrick Joseph Hackett and not Alan Brennan (a.k.a. William MacDonald) as first thought. The fingerprints identified the body, and the stab wounds and mutilation of the genitals linked the crime to the notorious serial killer, The Mutilator.

Capture, Trial & Imprisonment

An identical picture of MacDonald was circulated to every newspaper in the nation. MacDonald, now working on the Melbourne railways under another alias, "David Allan," was recognized by his workmates despite attempts to disguise himself by dying his hair and growing a mustache. Melbourne police arrested MacDonald on May

13, 1963, at Melbourne's Spencer Street railway station, where he worked as a railway employee. His capture brought an end to his reign of terror in Sydney and marked the conclusion of one of Australia's most notorious murder sprees.

During interrogation, MacDonald readily admitted to the killings, explaining to police that he had an uncontrollable urge to murder. He claimed that as a teenager, he was raped and felt compelled to disempower his victims, chosen at random. MacDonald, diagnosed with schizophrenia, stated that he heard voices telling him his victims were the corporal who raped him.

MacDonald was charged with four counts of murder and committed to stand trial on August 15, 1963. His trial began in September 1963 and was one of the most sensational in the nation. Pleading not guilty on the grounds of insanity, MacDonald testified in great detail about the murders. He described how blood sprayed over his raincoat as he castrated his victims, putting their genitals into plastic bags and taking them home. His graphic testimony caused some jurors to faint.

Despite overwhelming evidence of insanity, the jury found MacDonald guilty. Before passing sentence, Justice McLennan called it the most brutal case of murder and total disregard for human life he had encountered. MacDonald, showing no remorse, was sentenced to five consecutive life sentences with a strong recommendation that he never be released.

MacDonald was initially imprisoned at the Long Bay Correctional Centre and was placed in their hospital division. He was soon certified insane and transferred to a secure mental hospital.

Known simply as Bill in the prison system, he became institutionalized. In 2003, he stated, "I have no desire to go and live on the outside. I wouldn't last five minutes." At the age of ninety, William MacDonald was still in prison. He died from a gastrointestinal blockage on May 12, 2015, making MacDonald, at the time of his death, the oldest and longest-serving prisoner in custody in New South Wales.

SEVEN

Ivan Milat

THE BACKPACKER MURDERS

Ivan Robert Marko Milat was a serial killer from Australia who was dubbed "The Backpack Murderer." He was responsible for the abduction, assault, robbery, and murder of two men and five women in New South Wales between 1989 and 1992.

His crimes usually involved approaching backpackers along the Hume Highway, offering them transport to southern New South Wales. Once they accepted, he would take them into the Belanglo State Forest, where he would incapacitate and kill them. Milat is also suspected of committing numerous other similar offenses and murders across Australia.

These murders, characterized by extreme violence and sadism, left an indelible mark on Australian criminal history.

Background

Ivan Milat was born on December 27, 1944, in the Crown Street Women's Hospital in Guildford, New South Wales, to Croatian emigrant and laborer Stjepan Marko "Steven" Milat, 1902–1983 and Australian national Margaret Elizabeth Piddleston, 1920–2001. He was the fifth of their fourteen children.

The Milat family, struggling with poverty, lived in Bossley Park, thirty-six kilometers west of Sydney, in a rural weatherboard cottage farm but later moved to Liverpool. Despite their hardships, Milat's parents diligently raised, educated, and disciplined their children, sending them all to

Catholic schools. However, Steven Milat was known for his temper, exacerbated by alcoholism. The ten Milat boys, known to local police, often handled knives and firearms, spending afternoons shooting at targets in their parents' yards.

From a young age, Ivan Milat displayed antisocial and psychopathic behavior, such as attacking animals with machetes, which led to his placement in a residential school at age thirteen. By the time he was seventeen, he was in a juvenile detention center for theft and, at age nineteen, was involved in a store break-in, for which he received an eighteen-month prison sentence. A month after his release, he was caught driving a stolen car and sentenced to two years of hard labor. By September 1967, at age twenty-two, he received a three-year imprisonment sentence for theft.

After his release, on April 7, 1971, Milat abducted two eighteen-year-old female hitchhikers near the Liverpool railway station, raping one before they managed to escape at a petrol station café. He was arrested later that day and charged with rape and armed robbery.

While awaiting trial, he participated in a series of robberies with some of his brothers and faked his suicide by leaving his shoes at The Gap, a notorious Sydney suicide site. Authorities believe Milat fled to New Zealand, where he lived for two years. However, he was suspected of returning surreptitiously using a fake passport and living interstate to avoid detection.

When Milat's mother suffered a heart attack in 1974, he was arrested again, but the case against him would later be dismissed, and he went free. Milat then took a job as a truck driver for the traffic authority in 1975, where he would continue to work for the next twenty years.

In 1977, he unsuccessfully attempted to rape and murder two women hitchhiking from Liverpool to Canberra but was never charged.

Milat met sixteen-year-old Karen Duck in 1983, who was pregnant by Milat's cousin. The two started dating and were married one year later. They had a daughter of their own later. Karen and Milat constantly fought, and he often beat her. So she decided to leave him in 1987, and the couple was divorced in 1989.

The Backpacker Murders

While two joggers were out on their run on September 19, 1992, they discovered a corpse in the Belanglo State Forest. The following morning, police found a second body just 100 feet away from the first. Dental records quickly confirmed that the bodies were those of **Caroline Clarke** and **Joanne Walters**. Twenty-one-year-old Caroline and twenty-two-year-old Joanne were British backpackers last seen in Kings Cross on April 18, 1992. Joanne had been viciously attacked, being stabbed fifteen times, including in her neck and chest, and several times in her back. Caroline was shot ten times in the head at the burial site, and it is believed that she was used as target practice.

After an extensive search, investigators initially ruled out the possibility of further discoveries in the forest. However, on October 5, 1993, a local man searching for firewood found bones in a remote Belanglo section of the forest. Upon return with the police, two bodies were quickly discovered and identified as those of **James Gibson** and **Deborah Everist**, who went missing on December 30, 1989, after leaving Sydney for ConFest near Albury. James' skeleton, found in a fetal position, showed eight stab wounds. A large knife had severed his upper spine, causing paralysis. The other stab wounds also went through his back, which punctured his heart and lungs. Deborah had been viciously beaten, with fractures to her skull in two places, a broken jaw, and knife marks on her forehead. She had also been stabbed once in the back. Later, police would find James' camera and backpack over 75 miles north of where they found the body, at Galston Gorge.

On November 1, 1993, during a police sweep, a skeleton was discovered in a clearing along a fire trail in Belanglo. It was identified as that of **Simone Schmidl**, bearing at least eight stab wounds, two severing her spine and others puncturing her heart and lungs. Simone, a twenty-one-year-old German, had been missing since departing Sydney for Melbourne on January 20, 1991. Clothing found at the scene did not belong to Schmidl but matched that of another missing backpacker, Anja Habschied.

On November 4, 1993, the bodies of twenty-year-old **Anja Habschied** and her twenty-one-year-old boyfriend, **Gabor Neugebauer**, were found on a nearby fire trail in shallow graves 160 feet apart. They had disappeared on December 26, 1991, after leaving a hostel for Mildura. Anja's head had been removed, and even after several searches, it was never found. Gabor had been shot in the head six times. Medical examiners said that some of the victims did not die immediately and probably suffered terribly from the injuries they had.

The autopsy reports on some of the corpses showed evidence that some of the victims had been tortured.

Investigation

On October 14, 1993, police created a task force of more than twenty detectives to work on these cases. On November 5th, the New South Wales government increased the reward for information leading to the capture of the killer to A$500,000.

As the investigation progressed, police

developed a profile of the killer and faced an enormous volume of data from numerous sources. They applied link analysis technology, which narrowed the list of suspects from two hundred and thirty to a more manageable thirty-two. Speculation arose that because the victims had been attacked in pairs and usually killed in different ways, as well as buried separately, there was probably more than one killer responsible.

Twenty-four-year-old Paul Onions from the United Kingdom contacted the police on November 13, 1993. He had been backpacking in Australia a few years earlier, and on January 25, 1990, while hitchhiking from Liverpool station towards Mildura, he accepted a ride from a man known only as "Bill." South of the town of Mittagong and less than one kilometer from Belanglo, Bill pulled out a revolver and some rope, intending to rob Onions. Paul managed to flee while Bill shot at him. He managed to flag down a passing motorist, Joanne Berry from Canberra, and together, they reported the incident to the Bowral police, describing the assailant and his vehicle.

On April 13, 1994, investigators found the January 1990 report regarding the Onions' call about being attacked while hitchhiking. They also found corroborating statements written by Joanne Berry, the girlfriend of a man who worked with Ivat Milat. This breakthrough eventually led to the arrest and conviction of Milat, the man responsible for the backpacker murders.

Police surveillance of the Milat house had already begun on February 26, 1994. Investigators also discovered that Milat sold his silver Nissan Patrol shortly after the bodies of Caroline Clarke and Joanne Walters were found. Additionally, it was confirmed that Milat had not been working on the days of the attacks, and acquaintances informed police about Milat's obsession with weapons.

When the connection between the Belanglo murders and Paul Onions' experience was made, Onions flew to Australia to assist with the investigation, where he identified Milat as the man who had picked him up and tried to shoot him.

Arrest

On May 22, 1994, Milat was arrested for the attack and robbery of Onions at his house. Fifty police officers had surrounded his home. Police would find several weapons in the house, which included an Anschütz Model .22-calibre, a

1441/42 rifle, and parts of a .22-calibre Ruger 10/22 rifle, which was the same type of rifle used in both of the murders. They also found a Bowie knife and a Browning pistol, along with several items belonging to several of the victims. Police raided his mother's home as well as five of his brothers, where they found several things belonging to different victims.

On May 31st, Milat was charged with the seven backpacker murders. On June 28th, Milat sought legal aid to pay for his defense. Meanwhile, brothers Richard and Walter were tried because police found weapons, drugs, and stolen items on their properties.

Milat's trial started on March 26, 1996, in Sydney, prosecuted by Mark Tedeschi. Despite the overwhelming evidence against him, Milat was confident he would be found innocent. His defense argued that, despite the evidence, there was no proof of Milat's guilt. He even tried to blame other members of his family, particularly Richard. One hundred forty-five witnesses took the stand, including members of the Milat family who attempted to provide alibis. On June 18th, Milat took the stand himself, claiming his innocence.

After eighteen weeks of testimony, on July 27,

1996, Milat was found guilty of all seven murders and received seven life sentences with no chance of parole. The jury also found Milat guilty of the attempted murder, robbery, and false imprisonment of Onions, for which he received six years' imprisonment each.

Imprisonment & Appeals

On his first day at Maitland Gaol, Ivan Milat was beaten by another inmate, marking the beginning of his turbulent prison life. Nearly a year later, on May 16, 1997, Milat attempted to escape alongside convicted drug dealer and former Sydney councilor George Savvas. The escape plan failed, and Savvas was found hanged in his cell the following day. As a result, Milat was transferred to the maximum-security section at Goulburn Correctional Centre.

Milat appealed against his convictions in November 1997, citing a breach of his common law right to legal representation. Still, the New South Wales Court of Criminal Appeal dismissed his appeal. Milat was transferred to the High-Risk Management Corrections Centre (Supermax) at Goulburn Correctional Centre in 2001.

In 2004, Milat appealed to the High Court of

Australia, claiming new grounds. This appeal, too, was rejected. In his 2004 interview on *Australian Story*, Milat denied the involvement of any of his family in the seven murders of which he was convicted.

On October 27, 2005, the New South Wales Supreme Court refused Milat's final avenue of appeal. But that didn't stop him. In 2006, two additional application attempts were rejected. There was also a public outcry when it was revealed that Milat had been given a toaster and a television in his cell.

Milat used a plastic knife in prison to cut off his pinky finger on January 26, 2009, intending to mail it to the High Court of Australia to force an appeal. He was taken to the hospital under high security, but doctors decided surgery was not possible, and he was returned to prison the next day. This was not his first self-harm attempt, as in 2001, he swallowed razor blades, staples, and other metal objects.

Milet then went on a nine-day hunger strike in May of 2011, losing 25 kilograms in a failed attempt to be given a PlayStation. Another appeal attempt was denied in November 2011.

Milat was moved to the Prince of Wales Hospital in Randwick in May 2019, where he was diagnosed with terminal oesophageal cancer. Following his treatment, he was remanded to the Long Bay Correctional Centre to continue serving his sentence. Now terminally ill, in August of that year, Milat was transferred to a secure treatment unit at the Prince of Wales Hospital after losing 20 kilograms in previous weeks and exhibiting a high temperature. However, his condition was not deemed life-threatening at that time.

Death

Milat died on October 27, 2019, at 4:07 a.m. in the hospital wing at Long Bay Correctional Centre. He was seventy-four years old. Before his death, he wrote a letter to his family requesting that the New South Wales government pay for his funeral, a request that New South Wales Corrections Minister Anthony Roberts denied. Instead, his body was cremated with the costs reimbursed from his prison account.

In his final days, New South Wales Police made eight attempts to elicit a confession from Milat by visiting him in prison and the hospital. These attempts included using different combinations of detectives and recorded interviews with victims' families as investigative techniques. However, Milat provided no further information or confessions during these interactions. Although he never officially confessed, it is said that Milat told his mother that he was indeed responsible for the backpacker murders.

Other Potential Murders

Police still believe that Milat could have been involved in more murders than the original seven backpacker murders that he was convicted of. Serial killers usually start killing before their mid-thirties and not usually as late as Milat, who was forty-five with his first known murder in 1989. This typical pattern of serial killers led most profilers to believe that Milat was probably committing murders before then. Even one of Milat's brothers, Richard, claimed there were probably heaps of bodies out there still to be discovered. Milat had also worked as a truck driver since the nineteen seventies, which made him very mobile. All of these facts add to the speculation about him committing previous murders.

In 1993, a task force named "Task Force Air" was started to look into the unsolved deaths and disappearances of young people at the time. The investigations of that task force were revived and cross-referenced to Milat. They used Milat's previously known criminal modus operandi profile and applied it to the fifty-eight cold cases on file. The task force commander, Clive Small, thought that three of the unsolved murders on their list were likely to have been committed by Milat.

On February 26, 1971, pregnant mother **Keren Rowland** and her sister drove to Canberra in their cars and were supposed to meet at a motel there, but Keren never showed up. Later that night, her abandoned car was in an undeveloped town. On the following day, Milat bragged to his co-workers that he had murdered someone and buried their body under some bush.

Keren's remains were found only thirty feet from a trail in the Fairburn Pine Plantation near the Air Disaster Memorial outside of Canberra on May 3, 1971. Her cause of death was never established, and the murder scene was never preserved and is now blended in with Belanglo State Forest. At the time of her death, Milat worked for the Department of Main Roads, which meant he drove between Liverpool and Canberra frequently. He also drove a gold-colored Ford Fairmont – the exact vehicle that several witnesses had told police they saw following Keren around town the same evening she went missing. Her murder case remains open to this day.

On November 13, 1987, eighteen-year-old **Peter Letcher** was going to hitchhike to his Bathurst to see his parents but never showed up. His remains were found on January 21, 1988, in a ditch near the tourist center of Jenolan Caves. His body was entirely covered with branches and leaves, and he was lying face up. His hands were cuffed behind his back. Peter had been shot five times with a .22 caliber gun in the head. He was also stabbed several times in the back, with some evidence that he had been sexually assaulted. Just a few days before Peter disappeared, Milat had taken his estranged wife to the Jenolan Caves in the same area where Lechter's body was discovered.

On September 6, 1991, twenty-nine-year-old **Dianne Pennacchio** checked into the Lake George Hotel in Bungendore. She told a friend that she was going to hitchhike back to Queanbeyan. At around eleven that night, she left the hotel by herself and headed toward Kings Highway. A week later, when two forestry employees were in the Tallaganda State Forest, about forty kilometers south of Bungendore, they found Pennacchio's dead body lying face down. She had been stabbed through the spine of her back and then covered with branches and leaves in an attempt to hide her remains. Pennacchio was murdered during Milat's active murder spree.

Another series of unsolved disappearances of young women in the Hunter Region south of Newcastle was being considered. They were initially thought to be the responsibility of a separate unidentified serial killer. However, they became "of interest" to the task force for possibly being related to Milat.

Twenty-year-old **Leanne Goodall** was dropped off at the Muswellbrook railway station on December 30, 1978, by her brother so she could catch the train to Newcastle to visit with her parents, but she never made it there. Goodall wasn't reported to the police as missing until February 1979. Ivan Milat began road work in the area where Goodall disappeared in late 1978 and the first half of 1979.

On April 7, 1979, just after Goodall went missing, eighteen-year-old **Robyn Hickie** also disappeared. Hickie went out to catch the bus around seven that evening from a bus stop across the street from where she lived. Police initially thought she ran away from home and never searched for her. She was never seen again. A witness claimed to have seen Milat at the Belmont Hotel the night before Hickie vanished.

Amanda Robinson was last seen on her way home from a high school dance in Gateshead on April 21, 1979. Even though police thoroughly searched, she was never found, and the case was never solved. Sixteen-year-old **Amanda Zolis** was seen by her neighbor walking to the Hamilton bus stop on October 12, 1979. Later that evening, just after ten, Zolis called her father, telling him that she would visit a friend in Queensland but never made it there and has never been seen again. Eighteen-year-old **Annette Briffa** was last seen somewhere on the Pacific Highway hitchhiking towards Hornsby, where eyewitnesses saw her getting into an Orange Mazda on January 10, 1980. Twenty-two-year-old **Susan Isenhood** was reported missing by her family after her brother had dropped her off in the Mayfield neighborhood. Her remains would be found in 1986 in the Kiwarrak State Forest.

It wasn't until the task force was reviewing these cases in 2001 that Milat became a person of interest mainly because he was doing road work in the area when the murders happened. Milat had bragged to a friend that there were corpses in graves scattered around the area.

At trial, when Milat was testifying, he claimed to have picked up about fifteen hitchhikers in the region but had nothing to do with any of the children who had gone missing there. He even snapped back at the prosecutor, questioning why a fourteen-year-old like Amanda Robinson would be allowed to run around alone at midnight. However, he could not be charged with any of their disappearances as there was no physical evidence to link him to any of the victims.

The media has tried to link him to several other disappearances and murders. In the Summer of 1972, nineteen-year-old Anita Cunningham and eighteen-year-old Robyn Hoinville-Bartram, who shared an apartment in Melbourne, decided they wanted to go to Queensland. They were going to hitchhike their way there. Police discovered the half-nude body of Robyn underneath a bridge crossing Sensible Creek, which was about eighty kilometers from where she lived. She had been shot in the head with a .22 caliber rifle, which was the same type of rifle Milat used. Anita's body was never found, and like several of the other missing and murdered cases that happened around the area, there was no physical evidence to connect Milat to the case.

In October 1973, eighteen-year-old Gabrielle Jahnke and sixteen-year-old Michelle Riley wanted to hitchhike to the Gold Coast from Brisbane. About one week later, around the halfway mark, police found Gabrielle's body at the bottom of a steep hill off the side of the Pacific Highway, and Michelle's body was found nearby, covered with branches and leaves. Her dress had been pulled over her head, and her underwear was missing.

Twenty-one-year-old Lydia Notz, from Germany, was staying with a friend in Queensland on October 31, 1976. She left a note at the house saying she planned to return in a week. Two criminal psychologists who appeared on the Ivan Milat: Backpacker Murderer 2021 television show proclaimed that they believed Lydia Notz was likely the victim of Milat.

Twenty-one-year-old Narelle Mary Cox visited her friend who lived in Noosa, Queensland, on July 20, 1977. She disappeared from the same area that Milat was working – Brunswick Heads, New South Wales. Narelle's sister brought this to the attention of the Milat Task Force in 1994, but when they checked his work schedule, the dates didn't match, and they ruled him out. Later, the task force learned that Milat often had other employees sign in on the time sheet for him when he didn't show up for work – a practice that was quite common back then.

Twenty-two-year-old American Barbara Brown, who was dating a man from Melbourne, went missing from New South Wales on May 17, 1978. She was last seen when she left her boyfriend's brother's house to head to Queensland. She was planning to hitchhiking. In the television show *Ivan Milat: Backpack Murderer*, which aired in 2021, they claimed that Barbara's disappearance was at the hands of Milat.

Twenty-year-old Stephen Lapthorne was driving his girlfriend, eighteen-year-old Michelle Pope, home in his green Bedford on August 25, 1978, when the two of them vanished. Neither of their bodies or Stephen's car was ever found. Police believed they had gotten lost somewhere in the Chase National Park, and the case went cold. During the 2005 Milat task force inquiry, Milat was ruled the likely candidate responsible for the couple going missing. The Deputy State Coroner certified that both Lapthorne and Pope were deceased.

Twenty-two-year-old Alan Martin Fox and his girlfriend, seventeen-year-old Anneke Adriaansen, decided to hitchhike from their Byron Bay apartment to Kempsy. The couple left their apartment around noon on January 11, 1979, and were seen on Main Street in Byron Bay that afternoon. Milat was a possible suspect as he was working in the area around that time.

In the early evening of July 27, 1979, fifteen-year-old Toni Cavanagh and sixteen-year-old Kay Docherty were going to a local disco located in Wollongong. They were never seen again. Toni's parents received the couple's letter telling them they went to Sydney and would return home soon. After a couple of weeks and no word had been heard from them, the police were called, but the case was never solved. During the 2013 Milat task force investigation, Milat was considered a possible suspect. However, as in many previous cases, there was no evidence to prove it.

Seventeen-year-old Kim Cherie Teer was heading to Adelaide with her dog from East Melbourne, where she lived in September 1979. Kim often sent letters to her mother while traveling around the country. In one of her letters, she asked her mother to get her birth certificate for her so that she could get her driver's license. Kim didn't like hitchhiking to get to different places and wanted to learn to drive as she thought it would be safer. One day, the letters stopped coming, and Kim disappeared. When police were called back then to look into things, they figured that she probably met with foul play. The case was never solved.

Another teen couple, seventeen-year-old Elaine Johnson and eighteen-year-old Kerry Anne Joel, also went missing while trying to hitchhike on February 1, 1980, when they decided to travel to Wyong. Police at the time thought they must have encountered some danger on the road, but nothing was ever discovered. Milat was working in this region when this couple went missing.

Nurses Gillian Jamieson and Deborah Balken, both twenty, were last seen at the Parramatta tavern on June 12, 1980, having a drink and talking with a man who wore a wide-brimmed cowboy hat. Deborah's roommate got a phone call from her that same night where she said she was going to Wollongong with some friends for a party. At the time, Milat was working in the area, and police questioned him about the missing nurses. He was released as there was no evidence against him. The two nurses were later found dead, and the crime was never solved.

On April 20, 1981, twenty-one-year-old Joanne Lacey and her best friend, Lesley Toshak, hitchhiked from Sydney to Byron Bay to surf. Their bodies were later discovered, and their deaths were ruled suspicious.

On March 10, 1991, twenty-two-year-old Carmen Verheyden was last seen on the Hume Highway in Casula, hitchhiking sometime after midnight, just after she left a party. She was trying to get home but never made it. Police were suspicious of Milat possibly being involved in Carmen's disappearance, but they were unable to find any concrete evidence to link him to her.

Fourteen-year-old Melony Merrill Sutton and her sixteen-year-old brother, Chad Everett Sutton, were last seen by their mother when they left their home in Queensland at 8:35 a.m. on November 23, 1992, to walk to school. It was later discovered that the two were planning to hitchhike to Perth to look for their father. It is believed they walked through the Belanglo State Forest. They were never found.

Runs in the Family

On July 18, 2005, one of Ivan Milat's former lawyers, John Marsden, made a deathbed confession claiming that Ivan Milat and his sister, Shirley Soire, murdered two backpackers together who were traveling from Britain.

In November 2012, nineteen-year-old Matthew Milat, who was Ivan Milat's great-nephew, along with nineteen-year-old Cohen Klein, were both convicted for the murder of seventeen-year-old David Auchterlonie in November of 2010. While Matthew was beating Achterlonie with an axe, Cohen recorded the attack with his mobile phone. They were both given forty-three-year sentences to be served in prison.

In May 2015, homicide investigator Steve Aperen was questioning Milat's brother, Boris. Boris claimed that when Ivan was about seventeen, he told Boris that he had accidentally shot Neville Knight, a taxi driver, while trying to rob him back in March 1962. Neville was left paralyzed from the waist down from the shooting, and another man, Allan Dillon, was arrested, charged, and convicted of the crime and given a five-year prison sentence. Aperen gave both Dillon and Boris a polygraph test, which they both passed, convincing him that Ivan Milat shot Neville. However, there was insufficient evidence to arrest him for the crime.

EIGHT

Bandali Michael Debs

B andali Debs is a convicted Australian serial killer currently serving four life sentences plus an additional twenty-seven years for multiple murders, including the killing of two Victoria Police officers in 1998 and the 1997 murder of teenager Kristy Harty. Debs was initially detained at HM Prison Barwon in Victoria. On December 12, 2011, Debs was also convicted for the April 1995 shooting murder of New South Wales sex worker Donna Ann Hicks.

Background

Bandali Michael Debs was born Edmund Plancis on July 18, 1953. Not much is known about his childhood since he has avoided discussing his early years. However, a newspaper report in 2003 quoted his brother saying that they were tortured as children, although no firm evidence supports this claim. We do know that he was from Narre Warren, a southeastern suburb of Melbourne, and that he worked as a tiler who had five children, the youngest of whom, Joseph, died from a suspected drug overdose in December 2003 in Greensborough.

At his February 2003 trial for killing two police officers, **Sergeant Gary Silk** and **Senior Constable Rodney Miller,** in Moorabbin, Victoria, on August 16, 1998, Debs was convicted. He was sentenced to two life terms to be served consecutively without any chance of parole.

Twenty-two-year-old Jason Joseph Roberts, alleged to be an accomplice, was also convicted and sentenced to two consecutive life terms with a minimum of thirty-five years. However, his conviction was later quashed in July 2022 when a jury acquitted him.

Then, on June 20, 2005, Debs was charged with the murder of eighteen-year-old **Kristy Mary Harty**, who was killed on June 17, 1997. Kristy had been soliciting for sex along the Princes Highway when she met Debs. They drove to a secluded bush track in Upper Beaconsfield, where they had unprotected sex. She was later murdered by a single gunshot to the back of her head. Bushwalkers discovered her semi-naked body. DNA tests matched semen found on her body to Debs. At a trial in May 2007, Debs was convicted of Kristy Harty's murder and sentenced to a third consecutive life term.

Later, in 2008, Debs was linked to the April 1995 murder of **Donna Hicks**, who was shot to death in Sydney. She was last seen drinking at the Colyton Hotel and got into a four-wheel drive matching a Debs-owned vehicle. Debs was linked to her murder case through DNA analysis after being entered into a criminal DNA database. Homicide detectives interviewed Debs on September 30, 2008, then searched his home in Sydney. There was enough evidence to go to trial. On December 12, 2011, Debs was found guilty of murdering Donna Hicks in the New South Wales Supreme Court and received a fourth consecutive life term.

During Jason Roberts' 2022 retrial for the Silk–Miller police murders, Debs confessed to killing Donna Hicks. While imprisoned, Debs has undertaken various classes, including psychology, life skills, and computer training. He is employed as a prison carpet cleaner.

NINE

Leonard Fraser

THE ROCKHAMPTON RAPIST

L eonard Fraser was born in Ingham, Queensland, on June 27, 1951, and moved to Sydney in 1957. He quit school sometime in the 1960s and began committing crimes in 1966. At only fifteen, Fraser got his first prison sentence of one year after he was caught stealing things from other boys at the orphanage school he lived in at the time. Over the following years, Fraser was in and out of jail for theft and various other crimes.

Before receiving a life sentence for the kidnapping, sexual assault, and murder of nine-year-old **Keyra Steinhardt** in Queensland on September 7, 2000, Fraser spent twenty of the last twenty-two years in prison for raping various women. His criminal history included raping a female terminally ill cancer patient he was living with in early 1997.

Fraser was later charged with four additional murders. Police found numerous "trophies" he kept from his victims in his apartment, including ponytails from three different women that could not be traced to any of his known victims.

Initially, Fraser confessed to five murders in what appeared to be a deal with police to avoid the prison's general population. However, one of his alleged victims, fourteen-year-old Natasha Ryan, was later found alive and living with her boyfriend in a nearby town after being listed as missing for five years.

Despite inconsistencies in his confessions, Fraser's defense did not file for a mistrial. They also did not object to the prosecution using the same confession for three other victims, even though it included the false admission of Ryan's murder. The Ryan murder was also supported by testimony from a fellow prisoner who claimed Fraser had drawn detailed maps showing where Ryan's remains could be located.

Justice Brian Ambrose criticized the media for commenting on the value of confessions made to other prisoners in jail or the detectives under duress, which might have affected the trial.

Fraser was sentenced to three life sentences in June 2003 for the 1998 murders of **Sylvia Benedetti** and **Beverly Leggo**, as well as the 1999 manslaughter of **Julie Turner**. During the trial, the judge said that Fraser was a danger to the community and his cellmates because he was a sexual predator.

Fraser was held at the Wolston Correctional Centre until December 26, 2006, where he was taken to a hospital in Woolloongabba for chest pains. Fraser later died on January 1, 2007, of a heart attack.

TEN

John Wayne Glover

THE GRANNY KILLER

J ohn Wayne Glover was an Australian serial killer convicted of the murders of six elderly women from 1989 to 1990 in Sydney's North Shore. The fact that the victims were all older women led to Glover earning the nickname "The Granny Killer."

Following his arrest in 1990, he admitted to the murders and was sentenced to consecutive terms of life imprisonment without the possibility of parole.

He hanged himself in prison on September 9, 2005.

Background

John Wayne Glover was born on November 26, 1932, in Wolverhampton, England. He came from a working-class family and left school at fourteen. Glover had a troubled early life, marked by petty crimes dating back to 1947 when he was only fifteen. After he was caught stealing a purse, he was sentenced to twelve months in a boys' home. He enlisted in the British Army but was discharged after his criminal record was discovered.

Glover emigrated to Australia in 1956 or 1957 and lived in Melbourne before moving to Sydney, where he naturalized as an Australian citizen. Shortly after his arrival, he was convicted of robbery in both Victoria and New South Wales. In 1962, he was convicted on multiple counts of assaulting women, indecent assault, and theft, receiving a three-year good-behavior bond.

Glover had a complicated relationship with older women, particularly his mother, Freda, who had multiple husbands and boyfriends. After marrying Gay Rolls in 1968 and moving into his parents-in-law's home in Mosman, Sydney, his mother-in-law also became a source of tension. They had two daughters together.

Glover's mother moved to Australia in 1976 and died of breast cancer in 1989. Oddly, the same year, Glover himself was diagnosed with male breast cancer. Glover and his wife separated, and his wife took their daughters to New Zealand.

Despite his criminal background, Glover volunteered at the Senior Citizens Society and worked as a sales representative for the Four'N Twenty meat pie company. He was considered friendly and trustworthy by his friends and lived a seemingly contented lifestyle in Mosman.

Murders

Glover's killing spree began in 1989 when he was fifty-six years old. He targeted elderly women, and over fourteen months, he murdered six older women, including Winifreda, Lady Ashton, and the widow of English-Australian impressionist painter Sir Will Ashton. He attacked his victims with a hammer, strangled them with their pantyhose, and stole their money. His murders were opportunistic, with no apparent pattern other than the age and vulnerability of his victims.

On January 11, 1989, Glover attacked eighty-four-year-old **Margaret Todhunter**, stole her purse, and spent the money at the Mosman Returned and Services League club. Then, on March 1st, he attacked eighty-two-year-old **Gwendolin Mitchelhill** with a hammer in her apartment foyer, resulting in her death.

Two months later, on May 9th, Glover followed eighty-four-year-old **Lady Winfreda Ashton** to her apartment foyer, attacked her with a hammer, and strangled her with her pantyhose. Then, on November 2nd, he attacked eighty-five-year-old **Margaret Pahud**, hitting her with a blunt instrument and stealing her purse.

The next day, on November 3rd, Glover attacked eighty-one-year-old **Olive Cleveland** outside her retirement village, hitting her head on the concrete and strangling her. Also that month, on November 23rd, he attacked ninety-three-year-old **Muriel Falconer** at her home, hitting her with a hammer and strangling her with her undergarments.

Glover's final victim, sixty-year-old **Joan Sinclair**, was murdered on March 19, 1990. Police had Glover under surveillance by this time and entered Sinclair's home when they became concerned about the lack of movement. They found her body and Glover unconscious in a filled bathtub, having attempted suicide.

Trial & Imprisonment

Glover later admitted to the murders and was put on trial. He pleaded not guilty on the grounds of diminished responsibility, claiming a severe personality disorder. However, the Crown prosecutor argued he was aware of his actions, and he was found guilty. Glover was sentenced to a term of life in prison with no chance of parole. He was held at Lithgow Prison in a maximum-security cell.

In May 2005, Glover collapsed and was placed on suicide watch after expressing a desire to kill himself. Despite being monitored, Glover hanged himself in his cell on September 10, 2005.

Glover's case remains notorious in Australia. He was a seemingly ordinary man leading a double life as a brutal serial killer. His crimes and subsequent capture highlighted the hidden dangers faced by vulnerable members of the community. Later, the media depicted Glover's life and crimes in the telemovie *Underbelly Files: Tell Them Lucifer Was Here*, where Australian actor Greg Stone portrayed him.

ELEVEN

Caroline Grills

AUNTH THALLY

Caroline Grills was an Australian serial killer who poisoned her victims in the late 1940s and early 1950s. She was considered primarily a comfort killer – those who kill for material gain and a comfortable lifestyle. Usually, the victims of comfort killers are family members and close acquaintances. After a murder, a comfort killer will usually wait for some time to pass before killing again to allow any suspicions to subside. Caroline targeted wealthier members of her extended family to keep a respectable lifestyle, though her later murders had less clear motives.

Background

Caroline Mickelson was born between 1888 and 1890 in Balmain, Sydney, to Mary Preiers and George Mickelson. On April 22, 1908, she married Richard William Grills, and the couple had four sons. Caroline was a short woman who wore thick-rimmed dark glasses. She commonly served her friends and in-laws tea, cakes, and biscuits.

In 1947, Grills first came under suspicion after four family members died: her eighty-seven-year-old stepmother, **Christine Mickelson**, her relative by marriage and close family friend, **Angelina Thomas,** relative by marriage, **John Lundberg**, and her sister-in-law **Mary Anne Mickelson**.

On April 13, 1953, after two other family members became ill while staying with Grills, police tested the tea she served them. They found thallium in it, which was a common rat poison used at the time.

The police figured Grills murdered Christine Mickelson to inherit the house in Gladesville that Christine had inherited from Caroline's father. Similarly, her close family friend, Angelina Thomas, had left her holiday home in the Blue Mountains to Caroline and Richard Grills in her will.

Caroline was charged with four murders and three attempted murders in October 1953. The attempted murders included two other family members, John and Christine Downey, and Eveline Lundberg, Christine's mother.

On October 15, 1953, Caroline Grills was convicted and sentenced to death. After an appeal, the court commuted her sentence to life in prison. Inmates of Sydney's Long Bay Prison affectionately nicknamed her "Aunt Thally," a pun on "Aunt Sally."

Caroline Grills died from peritonitis caused by a ruptured gastric ulcer at Prince Henry Hospital in Randwick in October 1960. In the months following her death, more cases of thallium poisoning emerged, including the notable case of prominent Australian Rugby League footballer Bobby Lulham.

TWELVE

Edward Leonski

THE BROWNOUT STRANGLER

E dward Leonski was a United States Army soldier and serial killer who murdered three women in Melbourne, Australia, in 1942. He was dubbed "The Brownout Strangler." A "brownout" (or blackout in some countries) is an intentional or unintentional power outage. Melbourne had a wartime practice of reducing electricity voltage to conserve energy.

Melbourne police initially arrested Leonski for the murders, but because he was an American soldier, they sent him to an American military court to be tried. After his conviction in Military Court, he was sentenced to death and later executed. It was the first time that a citizen of another country was tried, convicted, and sentenced to death in Australia under the laws of their own country.

Background

Edward Joseph Leonski was born in Kenvil, New Jersey, on December 12, 1917. He was the sixth child of Russian-Jewish immigrants John Leonski, a laborer, and his Polish-born wife Amelia, née Harkavitz. He grew up in an abusive household with an alcoholic father who often beat him and his siblings. Leonski's older brother was committed to a mental institute before he had finished school.

Leonski joined the U.S. Army and trained for about one year. On February 2, 1942, after the U.S. entered World War II, he was transferred to

Melbourne, Australia, where the U.S. had set up a temporary military base.

Later, during his trial, the court's psychiatric examiner told the court that Leonski's mother had been overprotective and controlling. The psychologist further claimed that Leonski was bullied by neighborhood kids and called a mama's boy. The psychologist concluded that Leonski's crimes were a result of his resentment and hatred of his mother, constituting "symbolic matricide." Leonski confessed that his motive for the killings was a twisted fascination with female voices, particularly when they were singing, claiming he killed the women to "get their voices."

Murders

Forty-year-old **Ivy Violet McLeod** was found dead in Albert Park, Melbourne, on May 3, 1942. She had been beaten and strangled. Since she still had her purse, robbery was ruled out as a motive.

One week later, thirty-one-year-old **Pauline Thompson** was partying with friends at a club. A witness reported that they saw her talking to a man with an American accent. The next day, she was found strangled to death.

On May 18th, forty-year-old **Gladys**

Hosking was murdered on her walk home from her job at the University of Melbourne. A witness reported to the police that on the same night, a disheveled American man approached her for directions. He appeared out of breath and covered in mud. The description she gave matched the man seen with Pauline Thompson. It also matched descriptions given by other women who had survived recent attacks.

Investigation

It wasn't a lengthy investigation. The police started by looking into all the soldiers stationed at the American base in Melbourne. They had the American soldiers participate in a lineup and asked the survivors and witnesses of the attacks to see if they recognized anyone in the lineup. Several of the survivors positively identified twenty-four-year-old Leonski. Leonski, a private in the 52nd Signal Battalion, was arrested and charged with the three murders.

Trial & Execution

Leonski's crimes were committed in Australia, but the American Military Court conducted the trial.

Leonski admitted to committing the crimes, and the court convicted and sentenced him to death on July 17, 1942. American General Douglas MacArthur agreed and confirmed the sentence on October 14th. In a departure from standard procedure, MacArthur personally signed the execution order on November 4th instead of his staff signing it. And on November 9th, Eddie Leonski was hanged at HM Prison Pentridge.

Leonski's defense attorney, Lieutenant Ira C. Rothgerber Jr., a former Colorado lawyer, attempted to secure an external review, including one from the U.S. Supreme Court, but was unsuccessful.

Authorities would keep Leonski's remains at several of Australia's cemeteries until it was decided he would be permanently buried at the Schofield Barracks Post Cemetery in O'ahu, Hawaii, in Section 9, Row B, Site 8, which is a section reserved for prisoners of the military that died while in custody.

THIRTEEN

Arnold Sodeman

THE SCHOOLGIRL STRANGLER

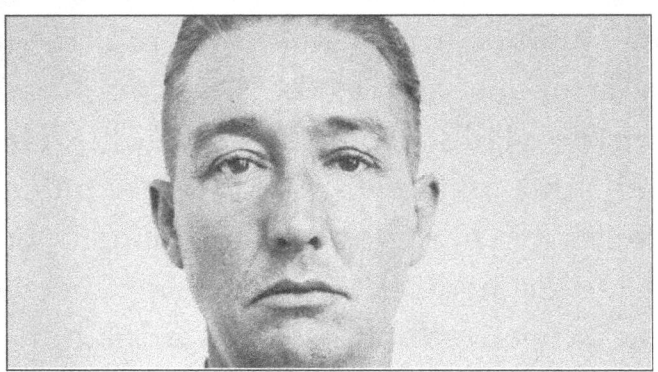

Arnold Karl Sodeman, also known as "The Schoolgirl Strangler," was an Australian serial killer who targeted children. He confessed to four killings before being executed at Pentridge Prison, Victoria, in 1936.

Sodeman was one of eleven people to be hanged at the prison.

Background

Arnold Sodeman was born in Victoria, Australia, on December 12, 1899. While he was growing up, his mother often suffered bouts of amnesia and was in and out of mental institutions. Mental illness seemed to run in their family, as both his father and grandfather died in mental hospitals.

At the age of eighteen, Sodeman committed a robbery and was sent to a reform school. Shortly after his release, he was caught robbing the Surrey Hills Railway Station. He also assaulted the manager. He was sentenced to three years of hard labor. He escaped but was caught. After he was returned, he received an additional twelve months of hard labor to his sentence.

When he was released, Sodeman moved to Melbourne. He had several temporary jobs in physical labor and construction. Eventually, he met Bernice Pope, and the two were married. In 1928, they had a daughter, Joan. Despite suffering from depression and frequent drunkenness, he was never violent towards his family and was considered hardworking, mild, and amiable, with a generous disposition.

Then something changed.

Murders

On November 9, 1930, Sodeman abducted a twelve-year-old schoolgirl, **Mena Griffiths**, from a local playground. He gave her friends money to buy ice cream and took Mena away under the pretext of running an errand. Her body was found two days later in an abandoned building in Ormond, strangled, gagged, and bound with her clothing.

A few months later, on January 10, 1931, Sodeman abducted sixteen-year-old **Hazel Wilson** and strangled her to death. Her body was also found in Ormond, similarly gagged and tied with her clothing.

Four years later, Sodeman struck again on January 1, 1935. He abducted and strangled twelve-year-old **Ethel Belshaw** in Inverloch. Belshaw had disappeared while intending to buy ice cream.

Sodeman killed his fourth victim, six-year-old **June Rushmer**, the daughter of a coworker, on December 1, 1945. June was taken from a local park, and her body was found the next day less than two kilometers from her Leongatha home. Witnesses reported seeing the child with a man on a bicycle shortly before her disappearance.

Investigation

Arnold Sodeman, a worker on a crew repairing roadways, became a suspect when a fellow worker jokingly mentioned seeing him near the crime scene. Sodeman's angry denial raised suspicion, and the police brought him in for an interview. Under questioning, he quickly confessed to the crimes. The police were initially skeptical but were eventually convinced by the detailed information he provided about the murders.

At the inquest into June Rushmer's death, the government pathologist reported that her hands were tied behind her back with cloth, a bloodstained garment was pushed into her mouth, and a piece of torn sock was tied around her neck. Witnesses testified seeing Sodeman near the scene, and he was committed for trial.

Trial, Imprisonment & Death

In February 1936, after a two-day trial, Sodeman was found guilty of murder. Despite testimony from medical professionals that he had a mental disorder causing uncontrollable impulses, the jury rejected the insanity defense.

Judge Charles Gavan Duffy sentenced him to death. An appeal to the Privy Council was unsuccessful.

Sodeman, who feared he might commit more murders if reprieved, spent his remaining time playing draughts with Edward Cornelius, another condemned prisoner.

Sodeman was hanged at Pentridge Prison on June 1, 1936. He was buried on the grounds of the prison in an unmarked plot. An autopsy revealed he was suffering from leptomeningitis, a condition that could cause severe brain congestion when aggravated by alcohol.

FOURTEEN

Derek Percy

Derek Percy was an Australian serial killer and convicted child killer linked to several mysterious deaths and disappearances of children during the 1960s. Even though he was only ever convicted of one murder, he was a suspect in many others, including the most infamous unsolved Australian murder cases of the 1960s — "The Wanda Beach Murders."

Background

Derek Ernest Percy was born on September 15, 1948, in Strathfield, New South Wales. He was the eldest of three sons born to Ernest and Elaine Percy. His father, a sailing enthusiast, worked as a New South Wales railway electrician before taking a job with the State Electricity Commission in Victoria. His work led to the family having to move multiple times, including Chelsea in 1954, Warrnambool in 1957, and Mount Beauty near Bright in 1961.

In 1964, at 16 years old, Percy caught the attention of authorities when he was caught stealing women's underwear for the first time. He admitted to wearing the underwear he stole as well as wearing dresses. But most disturbing was his admission that he used to cut up dolls into pieces, usually with a knife or razor blade.

The following year, in 1965, Percy's family moved to Khancoban, New South Wales. Around this time, Percy began to have violent sexual fantasies, and he journalled about them. He entered grade eleven after they moved to their new home but failed and had to repeat the year in school. Just after starting grade twelve, he quit school and joined the Australian Navy. He was trained in electrical mechanics and later stationed in a few locations until finally settling at the Cerebus Naval Base in 1969.

Murder

On July 27, 1969, Percy was arrested for the murder of twelve-year-old **Yvonne Tuohy** near Westernport Bay. He abducted Yvonne using a knife and also tried to kidnap her friend, eleven-year-old Shane Spiller. Shane was able to get away and later able to give the police a good description of the assailant and the car that he was driving.

Detectives drove around town with Shane, looking for the assailant. They found him at a laundromat, trying to wash the blood off his clothing from the attack. They arrested Percy, initially denying being involved in any attacks. Eventually, he admitted to the crime and took investigators to where he left Yvonne's body – about eight kilometers from where he abducted her.

When police searched his home, they found

his journal, which described several sexual fantasies, including cannibalism.

Percy was convicted of abduction and murder but found not responsible due to insanity. He was sent to a mental hospital for life.

Other Possible Crimes

During his examinations and therapy, Percy was unable to remember if he had committed any other crimes. He claimed to be unable to remember much about the previous few years. Doctors knew that he had pedophilic and psychopathic fantasies about children. The police had found more than thirty boxes containing several of his journals, maps, and newspaper clippings in a storage locker he had rented in Melbourne.

Given his deviancy, detectives suspected that perhaps Percy had committed other attacks, so they created an event calendar to track his travels before he was arrested to see if they could tie him to any other crime. After police were able to pinpoint all of the places that Percy had been, either from his enlistment in the army or vacations, he became a suspect in several missing children cases and other crimes against children.

Percy was stationed at the Sydney Harbor in May 1968, and there were child abductions around that time. On August 10th that year, seven-year-old Linda Stilwell was abducted and murdered while she was out playing. Percy said he could remember driving around the area but could not remember Linda Stilwell. In October 2014, a year after his death, Percy was formally ruled to have abducted and killed Linda.

Also, on April 1, 1969, a twelve-year-old girl was riding her bike near the base where Percy was stationed. He attempted to get her in his car, but she got away. She was later able to identify Percy after he had been arrested in the Yvonne Tuohy murder case.

The "Wanda Beach Murders" were the unsolved murders of fifteen-year-old Marianne Schmidt and Christine Sharrock at Wanda Beach in Sydney, New South Wales, on January 11, 1965. The victims were best friends who simply went to the beach one day. Sadly, their partially buried bodies were discovered the next day. The brutal nature of the slayings brought massive publicity to the case. By April 1966, it was the largest investigation in Australian history. Police had interviewed some 7,000 people. It remains one of the most infamous unsolved

Australian murder cases of the 1960s. Percy was considered a leading suspect. But while he can be linked to Cronulla on the date of the murders, no other links have been found. It was hoped he would confess on his deathbed, but it didn't come.

Before admitting to any more crimes and murders, Percy died of lung cancer. He was sent to the St. Vincent Hospital in Melbourne on July 23, 2013, where he died. At the time, he was the longest-serving inmate at forty-four years.

FIFTEEN

Lindsey Robert Rose

L indsey Robert Rose is a serial killer currently serving five life sentences without parole for the murders of five people between 1984 and 1994. He was born Lindsey Robert Lehman on May 2, 1955, in North

Sydney, New South Wales, Australia. He was raised by his mother, who had separated from his father before his birth. Lindsey took his stepfather's surname after his mother remarried.

After Rose finished school in 1976, he worked for the New South Wales Ambulance Service. He worked that job for three years until he got his private investigator's license in 1979. His criminal career started after that.

Murders

Rose shot **Edward John Cavanagh** to death in his Sydney home on January 20, 1984. The motive, apparently, was revenge. Cavanagh had severely beaten up a friend of Rose's the previous year. Rose also shot Cavanagh's girlfriend, **Carmelita Lee**, to death as she was a witness to his crime. Edward Cavanagh ran a trucking business and was alleged to have ties with the Calabrian mafia, including the notorious drug lord Robert Trimbole.

On January 19, 1987, Rose broke into a luxury home belonging to wealthy businessman William

Graf. He thought nobody was home and had intended merely to rob the place. As it was, William's girlfriend, **Reynette Holford**, was there. When she walked in on him, Rose was surprised. In a panic, he used the screwdriver he had with him and a knife from the house to stab her several times before tying her up and leaving. Reynette died from the attack.

On February 14, 1994, Rose murdered **Fatma Ozonol** and **Kerrie Pang** at Kerrie's Oasis, a massage parlor. Kerrie, the owner of the business, was the intended victim. Fatma was just in the wrong place at the wrong time. Rose shot and killed Fatma first and then shot and stabbed Kerrie until she was dead. The murder of Kerrie was arranged by her de facto partner, Mark Lewis, who was dissatisfied with her line of work and had issues in their relationship. Rose was hired to kill her.

A friend of Rose's, Ronald Waters, was offered $500 to assist him by knocking on the door of the massage parlor to gain access since Kerrie knew who Rose was. Ronald was unaware of Rose's lethal intentions and never received the payment.

Mark Lewis was later found guilty of both murders and sentenced to life imprisonment without parole for Kerrie's murder and eighteen years for Fatma's murder. Ronald Waters was sentenced to an eighteen-month prison term after pleading guilty to being an accessory after the fact of the crime.

Investigation

It wasn't until 1996 that Rose became a suspect in any of the five murders, not until a crooked police officer who had illegal dealings with Rose got in trouble. He told detectives that Rose was bragging about committing murder. He was questioned and surveilled; however, he escaped.

Rose packed some clothes and drove from Sydney to Adelaide on July 4, 1996. Using his birth name, Lindsey Lehman, he got a job and decided to remain there. It was about ten months before the police caught up with him. After a program aired on television on April 9, 1997, that featured Rose and showed his mugshot, a fellow employee recognized him. The employee reported to the police. He was arrested the next day.

Trial & Imprisonment

On June 18, 1998, Rose was formally charged with five counts of murder. He pleaded not guilty. The trial lasted the whole summer, and he was convicted of all five charges on September 3, 1998. After that, he was sentenced to five life sentences with no chance of parole. Three months later, he received an additional thirty-nine years in prison for various charges, including selling drugs, kidnapping, robbery, and interfering in a criminal investigation.

Rose was among the first inmates to be sent to the new Supermax prison in 2001. He didn't like being at this prison, not because it was disciplined and had strict rules, but because there were a lot of other prisoners there who were Islamic or converting to Islam. He was so bothered by this that he even sent letters to the prison authorities offering to help stop inmates from becoming Islamic in faith. Rose was also sending letters complaining about how bad the conditions were at the prison, including the fact that they did not have a library or any chance to learn any skills there.

SIXTEEN

Bradley Robert Edwards

THE CLAREMONT KILLER

Bradley Robert Edwards is an Australian serial killer behind a series of murders called "The Claremont Serial Killings" that occurred between 1996 and 1997. Three women disappeared after socializing with friends at clubs in Claremont, a wealthy western suburb of Perth, Western Australia. Two of those women were found murdered, and one has never been found. The similarities in the circumstances of their disappearances and murders led police to suspect the involvement of a serial killer dubbed "The Claremont Killer." This case became the state's largest, longest-running, and most expensive investigation.

In 2016, nineteen years after the murders, Bradley Edwards was finally arrested after improvements in DNA tied him to the murders. His trial lasted seven months with over two hundred witnesses, and on September 24, 2020, he was found guilty of two of the murders and not guilty of one. He was sentenced to a term of life in prison with a minimum of forty years.

Background

Not much is known about Bradley Robert Edwards. He opted not to give evidence during his seven-month trial and declined to participate in any psychiatric evaluations.

We know he was born in Western Australia on December 7, 1968. We know that he worked as an electrician at Telstra and that it was alleged he used company vehicles after hours to commit the crimes.

We know that he started attacking women as early as 1988. DNA proved he assaulted an eighteen-year-old woman on February 15th of that year, breaking into her Huntingdale home and assaulting her as she slept. He also tried to rape a social worker at Hollywood Hospital on May 7, 1990. He admitted to this at the time it happened and received probation. Then in 1995, he raped a seventeen-year-old teenager after abducting her from Claremont and bringing her to the nearby Karrakatta cemetery.

The attack on the woman in Huntingdale provided the crucial piece of evidence homicide detectives needed to arrest him almost twenty-nine years later because he left behind a semen-stained silk kimono. When it was finally tested in November 2016, the DNA matched swabs taken from the teenager he abducted and raped in 1995 and DNA under the fingernails of one of the murder victims.

Murders

On January 27, 1996, eighteen-year-old **Sarah Spier** left a club in Claremont just after closing time, around two in the morning, walked to a payphone, and called a cab to pick her up. A few minutes later, she was no longer there when the taxi came to pick her up. Later, three witnesses said they saw Spiers getting into a car at that location. After she was reported missing, the story became big news.

A little more than four months later, on June 9, 1996, twenty-three-year-old **Jane Rimmer** was out with friends in the same part of town. Jane and her two girlfriends had socialized and drank in two hotels that evening and decided to go to a bar around midnight. When they arrived and saw the long lineup, her friends called it a night and took a cab home. However, Jane decided to stay. She was last seen waiting outside the bar by herself on the security footage from one of the hotels. Almost two months later, on August 3, 1996, her naked body was found in the woods by a family picking wildflowers in a park in Wellard.

Nine months later, on March 15, 1997, twenty-seven-year-old lawyer **Ciara Glennon** also vanished from the same Claremont area the others had. Ciara was socializing with her friends and having drinks at the Continental Hotel. A little after midnight, she decided to make her way home. Witnesses later told police that they remembered seeing her at a bus stop around midnight and noticed a light-colored car pulled up beside her. It looked like she talked to the driver for a while before getting into the car and leaving. Ciara's semi-clothed body was found three weeks later in a small park about forty kilometers north of where she disappeared.

Investigation

When Sarah Spiers disappeared in January 1996, the Major Crimes Squad took over the investigation within forty-eight hours. When Jane Rimmer disappeared four months later, the Western Australia Police established a special task force called "Macro" to investigate the two similar cases. After Ciara Glennon went missing, police admitted to the press that they were now looking for a serial killer in the area. They were offering a reward of a quarter of a million dollars for any information leading to the killer's arrest.

Initially, suspicion centered on unidentified vehicles seen at two locations and an unnamed man in video footage. Then, the focus shifted to Perth's taxi drivers since the women each had called for a taxi to pick them up after leaving the bar.

Thousands of taxi drivers licensed in Western Australia were fingerprinted and asked to take a DNA test in a massive testing exercise. Many unlicensed taxi drivers were discovered through the testing, resulting in the raising of standards for eligibility. Seventy-eight taxi drivers lost their licenses because of their significant criminal histories. Stricter standards were also applied after that, and decommissioned taxis were stripped of their insignia and equipment.

In December 2015, investigators revealed that fibers found on Jane Rimmer matched those of a vehicle that was seen the same night she went missing by witnesses.

The task force kept details known about the injuries and deaths of the victims to themselves during the investigation. They also used several tactics that stirred some controversy. For example, when they sent one hundred and ten possible suspects a questionnaire that asked direct questions such as, "Are you the Killer?" Or when they accepted an offer by serial killer David Birnie to assist in the investigation. The task force was closed in Fall 2005, and the Special Crimes Squad of the police department took over handling the investigation.

Suspects

Early suspects included Lance Williams, a forty-one-year-old public servant from Cottesloe. He became the prime suspect in the Claremont serial killings after his behavior attracted police attention. Williams was observed driving around the Claremont area up to thirty times after midnight during a decoy operation. Subject to extensive surveillance and police pressure over several years, Williams consistently maintained his innocence. Finally, in 2008, police ruled him no longer a person of interest after six interrogations.

Police considered Bradley Murdoch for a while until it was determined that he was in jail at the time of the murders.

Mark Dixie became the prime suspect in October 2006, and police ordered his DNA sample. However, after a thorough investigation, detectives also ruled out him.

Bradley Robert Edwards was brought in for questioning on December 22, 2016. He became a person of interest after police connected him with other assaults on females in the area. They had his fingerprints from his prior assault on a social worker at Hollywood Hospital on May 7, 1990. His fingerprints matched fingerprints found at a break-and-enter and assault in 1988. So they asked him to come in. The day after they interrogated him, he was formally charged with the murders of Jane Rimmer and Ciara Glennon.

Edwards was subsequently charged with breaking and entering and unlawful detention of an eighteen-year-old unnamed Huntington woman on February 15, 1988. His DNA matched the DNA found on the kimono left as the assailant fled the scene. He was also charged with aggravated sexual assault with penetration without consent of the unnamed seventeen-year-old girl from Claremont on February 12, 1995, after his DNA matched the DNA taken from her when it happened.

Later, on February 22, 2018, Edward was charged with the murder of Sarah Spiers, who police believe was his first murder victim.

Trial

The prosecution asked for Edwards to be tried by a judge only, without any jury, because of the amount of publicity the case was getting and the graphic nature of the discovered evidence. This motion was approved, and the trial began on November 25, 2019.

During the trial, the court heard that two of the victims had defensive wounds. Edwards' DNA was found under Ciara Glennon's fingernails, which matched the DNA on a kimono linked to another crime. The defense argued that this evidence was contaminated in the laboratory.

A significant piece of evidence was related to the Telstra work vehicles. Edwards, who worked as a technician at the time, was alleged to have used company vehicles after hours to commit the crimes. This claim was supported by a security guard who recalled seeing a Telecom van parked multiple times at Karrakatta Cemetery "for no apparent reason," both after the 1995 attack and before Sarah Spiers' disappearance. The prosecution, led by Carmel Barbagallo, presented this evidence as part of a case called the "Telstra Living Witness Project," which involved reports of a man with a Telstra station wagon stopping to look at women and offering them rides between 1995 and 1997.

During the trial, a witness from a group of men known as the "Burger Boys" identified a Series 1 VS Commodore station wagon with distinctive teardrop hubcaps cruising past them shortly after Ciara Glennon walked by. Between April 1996 and December 1998, Edwards had driven the same kind of vehicle. His vehicle was tracked down and impounded on the same day as his arrest. The hearing revealed that fibers matching the carpet in the rear of Edwards' vehicle were found on the bodies of both Jane Rimmer and Ciara Glennon. The defense argued that these fibers could have come from another source or that the car wasn't registered with the Western Australian government.

The trial lasted seven months, with over two hundred witnesses testifying and over six hundred pieces of evidence shared. On June 25, 2020, it was finally over. Justice Hall retired to deliberate, indicating that the verdict might be delivered before Edwards' remand in custody ended.

On September 24, 2020, Hall handed down a six hundred-and-nineteen-page written verdict, finding Edwards guilty of the murders of Jane Rimmer and Ciara Glennon but not of Sarah

Spiers. However, he noted it was "more likely" than not that Edwards was involved in her disappearance. The Judge sentenced him to life imprisonment with the possibility of parole after forty years on December 23, 2020.

It has been argued that Sarah Spiers might not have been the Claremont Serial Killer's first victim. Journalist Liam Bartlett suggested that the police informed the father of Julie Cutler, a twenty-two-year-old university student from Fremantle, that his daughter was likely another victim. Cutler vanished after leaving a staff function at the Hilton Hotel in Perth at 9:00 p.m. on June 20, 1988. Her car was discovered in the surf near the groin at Cottesloe Beach two days later, but her fate remains unknown.

Other possible victims included nineteen-year-old Lisa Brown, a sex worker who disappeared on November 10, 1998, and Sara McMahon, a twenty-year-old who vanished on November 8, 2000.

SEVENTEEN

John Bunting

THE SNOWTOWN MURDERS

T he "Snowtown Murders," or the "Bodies in Barrels Murders," were a series of murders that happened between August 1992 and May 1999 in or around the city of Adelaide, South Australia. John Bunting, Robert Wagner, and James Vlassakis were later convicted of these crimes, and Mark Haydon was sentenced for helping with the disposal of the bodies. The trial became one of Australia's most publicized trials ever.

Most of the victims' bodies were discovered in barrels within an abandoned bank vault in Snowtown, South Australia, which led to the media referring to the case by these names. Interestingly, only one of the victims was killed in Snowtown, located approximately 140 kilometers north of Adelaide. Neither the twelve victims nor the three principal perpetrators were from the town.

While the exact motivation for the murders remains unclear, it is known that John Justin Bunting was the leader of the group. He led the rest of the killers to believe their victims were pedophiles, homosexuals, or "weak." In several instances, the murders were preceded by acts of torture, and there were attempts to take over the victims' identities, social security payments, and bank accounts.

Initially, the infamy surrounding the murders brought a temporary economic boost to Snowtown due to an influx of curious tourists. However, this notoriety eventually created a lasting stigma, leading authorities to consider changing the town's name and identity. The case has been detailed in numerous books and made into a 2011 movie called *Snowtown*.

Perpetrators

John Justin Bunting was found to be the leader of the group. He was born in Inala, Queensland, on September 4, 1955. At eight years old, Bunting was beaten and sexually assaulted by a friend's older brother. As a result, he developed an intense hatred of pedophiles and homosexuals. He reportedly enjoyed weaponry, photography, and anatomy. At twenty-two-years-old, Bunting worked at an abattoir and bragged about slaughtering animals. In 1991, he moved to Salisbury North, South Australia, where he met and became friends with his new neighbors and future partners-in-crime, Mark Haydon and Robert Wagner.

After Bunting was convicted and placed in Broadmoor Hospital in Britain, he was analyzed by a forensic psychiatrist there, Kevin Howells. He was diagnosed as a psychopathic killer who lacked any emotions or empathy. He also derived his satisfaction from the control over his victims. Bunting would often make his victims call him by a title such as "Master," "God," "Lord," "Sir," or even sometimes, "Chief Inspector."

Robert Joe Wagner was born on November 28, 1971, in Parramatta, New South Wales.

James "Jamie" Spyridon Vlassakis was born on December 24, 1979, and lived with Bunting, his mother, and his half-brother. He was gradually drawn into the murders, helping to torture and kill his half-brother, Troy Youde, and his stepbrother, David Johnson. Vlassakis confessed to four murders in 2001 and became a key witness for the Crown by providing information that helped to prosecute both Bunting and Wagner. Vlassakis was placed in an undisclosed prison for his protection after he was sentenced to a twenty-six-year prison term.

Elizabeth Harvey, Vlassakis' mother, was aware of some of the murders and even helped in one of them. She died from cancer shortly after the others were arrested.

Mark Haydon, born on December 4, 1958, pleaded guilty to helping the serial killers dispose of some of the bodies.

Crimes

The victims of the Snowtown murders were chosen arbitrarily by John Bunting for imagined infractions. Some were targeted because Bunting suspected them of being pedophiles, often based on flimsy evidence or rumors. Others were killed due to Bunting's dislike of obese people, drug users, or homosexuals. Most of the victims were chosen from people that at least one of the group members knew. It could have been a friend, a roommate, a coworker, or even a family member that was chosen.

In a spare room in his house, Bunting created a "rock spider wall," which was just a chart of names of the people who he believed were either pedophiles or homosexuals. He would go into the room, select a name, and then call them, giving them a warning that they were going to get what was coming to them for being a pedophile or whatever he deemed to be their punishable offense.

The murderers often stole their victims' social security and bank details to impersonate them after their deaths and to continue collecting their pensions. Although a total of $97,200 was collected this way, social security fraud is not believed to have been the primary motive for the murders.

Victims

Twenty-year-old **Clinton Douglas Trezise** was invited to John Buntings for a drink on August 31, 1992. After they had a few drinks, Bunting called Clinton "Happy Pants" and accused him of being a pedophile. Then Bunting grabbed a shovel and hit him over the head several times until he was dead.

Clinton was found buried in a shallow grave on August 16, 1994, at Lower Light, South Australia. Bunting later boasted to Vlassakis about the murder, revealing that he had disposed of Clinton's body with Wagner and Lane's assistance.

Twenty-six-year-old **Ray Allan Peter Davies** was an intellectually disabled man who was having a sexual relationship with Suzanne Allen, Bunting's ex-girlfriend. Both of Suzanne's grandsons told Bunting that Davies had made sexual advances toward them. The inappropriate situation led to the end of Suzanne and Ray's relationship; however, they remained friends, and he was residing in a camper in her backyard.

On the evening of December 26, 1995, Bunting and Allen were seen taking things from Ray's camper, and Blunting later told Vlassakis that he had murdered Ray the day before (Christmas Day) after Elizabeth Harvey had stabbed him in his leg and Robert Wagner had tried to strangle him. On May 26, 1999, Ray Davies' body was found on one of Bunting's old properties.

On May 23, 1999, forty-seven-year-old **Suzanne Allen** was found buried at Bunting's house in Salisbury, wrapped in eleven different plastic bags. Bunting continued to collect her pension after her death, claiming she had died of a heart attack. Murder charges regarding Suzanne's death were eventually dropped due to lack of evidence. It is uncertain exactly when she was murdered, but it was most likely after she helped clear out Ray Davies' camper.

Nineteen-year-old **Michelle Gardiner**, also known as Michael Gardiner, was a transgender woman who lived with Nicole Zuritta, a cousin of Wagner's wife. Bunting called her "The Biggest Homo." Michelle always played with Wagner's children, which infuriated him. She disappeared in September 1997. Wagner and Bunting, together, drove Michelle out to the Murray Bridge, strangled her, and placed her body in a large barrel. It was eventually placed in the Snowtown Bank vault, where it was found later on May 20, 1999.

Forty-two-year-old **Vanessa Lane**, formerly known as Barry Lane, was Wagner's ex-partner. Bunting accepted Vanessa into his circle because she kept him informed about local pedophiles. After Vanessa was accused of molesting a boy, her house was firebombed, and Wagner left her. Vanessa was later tortured for information about her bank accounts and then strangled to death on October 17, 1997. Her dismembered body was found in a barrel in the Snowtown bank vault on May 20, 1999.

Eighteen-year-old **Thomas Eugenio Trevelyan**, Vanessa Lane's last partner, had paranoid schizophrenia. He helped Bunting and Wagner kill Vanessa. On November 5, 1997, Thomas was driven to Kersbrook in the Adelaide Hills, forced to lean against a box with a noose around his neck, and found hanging from a tree the next day. The coroner ruled his death a suicide.

Twenty-nine-year-old **Gavin Allan Porter**, a friend of Vlassakis, was a diagnosed schizophrenic. He moved to Adelaide in 1997 and lived with Vlassakis. Bunting decided Gavin should be the next victim after a used syringe left by Gavin pricked him. He was strangled while sleeping in his car sometime late in 1997, and his body was found in a barrel on May 20, 1999.

Twenty-one-year-old **Troy Youde** was James Vlassakis' half-brother who had sexually abused him. One night, Bunting and Wagner woke Vlassakis to tell him they were going to kill Youde. They beat and tortured Youde, demanding his financial information before strangling him. His body was also found in a barrel on May 20, 1999.

Eighteen-year-old **Frederick "Fred" Robert Brooks**, the son of Jodie Elliott and nephew of Elizabeth Haydon, was accused by Bunting of inappropriate behavior with young girls. In September 1998, Fred was tortured in a bathtub, subjected to various cruel acts, and eventually killed. His body was found in a barrel in the Snowtown bank on May 20, 1999.

Twenty-nine-year-old **Gary O'Dwyer**, a mentally and physically disabled neighbor of Bunting, was targeted for his disability benefits. In October 1998, O'Dwyer was tortured and killed. His body was placed in a barrel and found in the Snowtown bank vault on May 20, 1999.

Thirty-seven-year-old **Elizabeth Haydon**, Mark Haydon's wife, was killed because she knew about the murders. On November 21, 1998, Bunting and Wagner tortured and killed her, placing her body in a barrel. Elizabeth's body was found in the Snowtown bank vault on May 20, 1999.

Twenty-four-year-old **David Johnson**, Vlassakis' stepbrother, was disliked by Bunting for his cleanliness and appearance. On May 9, 1999, Vlassakis lured him to the Snowtown bank to buy a computer. David was overpowered and killed. His body was found with the others on May 20, 1999. During questioning, it was revealed that Bunting and Wagner fried and ate a piece of Johnson's flesh.

Investigation

Clinton Trezise's body was found at Lower Light in 1994, but no connection to John Bunting was made right away. Thomas Trevilyan's death in 1997 was initially treated as a suicide. So, it was the police inquiries into Elizabeth Haydon's disappearance that led them to Snowtown and, ultimately, John Bunting.

On May 20, 1999, the South Australian Police discovered the remains of eight victims in six plastic barrels in a disused bank vault. It is believed that the killers moved the bodies around after they became aware of the police investigation. They suspect they had been held in several locations in South Australia before being moved to Snowtown in 1999. The discovery led to the murders being dubbed the "Bodies in Barrels Murders" and "The Snowtown Murders," even though only one murder occurred in Snowtown.

Police arrested and charged Bunting, Wagner, and Haydon with two murders after two bodies were discovered in the backyard of Bunting's Adelaide house on May 21, 1999. James Vlassakis was arrested on May 26, 1999, while living in Bunting's home. He confessed to four murders and became a key witness for the Crown by providing information that helped to prosecute both Bunting and Wagner.

Trial

John Bunting and Robert Wagner's trial would be the lengthiest in Australian history, lasting twelve months and closing in December 2003. The jury convicted Bunting of eleven murders and Wagner of ten murders. Mark Haydon was convicted of the four murders that he had earlier pleaded guilty to and, in the following year, was convicted of assisting in five of the other murders that the other members of the group committed.

As the judge on the case considered Bunting to have been in charge and directed all of the murders, he was sentenced to eleven life terms to be served consecutively in prison with no possibility of parole. The judge also sentenced Wagner to ten life sentences, to be served consecutively and without a chance for parole.

In 2004, James Vlassakis was sentenced to four life terms to be served consecutively and without any possibility of parole. Mark Haydon was given a twenty-five-year sentence with a minimum of eighteen years to be served before applying for parole.

Mark Haydon was granted parole in February 2024 for good behavior and released in April. He was ordered to live in a halfway house in Adelaide.

Aftermath

The house where Bunting lived and buried bodies in Salisbury was demolished. The bank they also used was sold at an auction and is now a new business run by new owners. A memorial plaque has been placed in clear view so anyone entering the company can see it.

Since the Snowtown murders, the small farming town has become a grim destination for tourists seeking to explore the dark stories associated with the crimes. Snowtown, still a quaint farming town, has become a landmark associated with the twelve murders committed in the 1990s. Tourists often visit Snowtown because of the murders, overlooking other issues facing the town. As the true crime industry has grown in popularity, Snowtown has become increasingly well-known, adding pressure on the community. With a decline in economic opportunities, the population of Snowtown continues to grapple with ongoing trauma and social stigma.

EIGHTEEN

Carl Williams

MELBOURNE BABYFACE KILLER

Carl Williams was a convicted Australian murderer and drug trafficker who was dubbed the "Melbourne Babyface Killer." He was a central figure in the Melbourne gangland killings, and he ultimately became their final victim. Williams enlisted the help of others to carry out contract killings in exchange for large sums of cash.

Williams was sentenced to life imprisonment with a non-parole period of thirty-five years for ordering the murder of three people and conspiring to murder a fourth. Had he lived, Williams would not have been eligible for parole until he was seventy-one years old.

On April 19, 2010, Williams was beaten to death with an exercise bike arm while in the gym at HM Prison Barwon by fellow inmate Matthew Charles Johnson.

Background

Carl Anthony Williams was born on October 13, 1970. He attended Broad Meadows Technical School in the 1980s, leaving in Year 11. He spent much of his childhood in Western Melbourne with his friends. Carl's older brother, Shane, died from a heroin overdose in 1997.

Williams was married to Roberta Mercieca, a convicted drug trafficker, with whom he had one daughter, Dhakota, born on March 10, 2001. Before turning to crime, he held various laboring jobs and opened a children's clothing store with his wife. But it eventually failed.

Williams' first drug charge came in November 1999, when he, his father, George, and another acquaintance were arrested and charged with drug trafficking in Fir Close, Broadmeadows. They had an illegal drug-making factory, and during that arrest, police seized about twenty million dollars worth of amphetamines.

Even though his first drug charge was in 1999, he was involved in criminal activities long before that. In May 1990, he was fined $400 for handling stolen goods, possessing stolen property, and failing to answer bail. In March 1993, he was sentenced to 150 hours of community work for criminal damage and throwing a missile. By December 1994, he was sentenced to 12 months imprisonment, with six months suspended for two years, for attempting to traffic in a drug of dependence.

In 2002, Williams met Andrew Veniamin through a mutual friend, Tony Mokbel. Veniamin became Williams' right-hand man until he was shot and killed on March 25, 2004.

By April 2004, Carl Williams was so infamous that, under the Casino Control Act, the police banned him from any Crown Casinos. It is not precisely known why he was banned. Most likely, it was because wherever Carl Williams went, shootouts and violence followed. It was rumored that the police were trying to get him banned from other public establishments as a matter of public safety.

The Melbourne Gangland Killings

On October 13, 1999, Williams was shot in the abdomen by Jason Moran over an $80,000 debt owed to the Moran family. This incident ignited a prolonged underworld conflict known as "The Melbourne Gangland Killings."

On June 15, 2000, **Mark Moran** was shot dead in his home. Williams was charged with Morgan's murder, but later, the charges were dropped in exchange for him pleading guilty to other murders he committed.

On the morning of June 21, 2003, **Jason Moran** and **Pasquale Barbaro** were both shot to death while sitting in their van in a hotel parking lot in Melbourne. They were there with five of their children to see a football game, but before they could get out of the van, the killer walked up and shot them both in front of the carload of kids.

The gunman, Victor Brincat, after he was arrested, told police that Carl Williams had paid him to kill Moran and Barbaro. Williams was initially charged with the murders, but after he made a deal with prosecutors to confess to other murders, the charges were dropped.

Mark Mallia, an associate of the murdered underworld criminal Nik Radev, was found dead on August 18, 2003. Firefighters responding to a fire in a stormwater drain in Sunshine discovered a wheelie bin containing Mallia's charred remains.

On October 25, 2003, **Michael Marshall** was shot outside his home in South Yarra in front of his five-year-old son.

On March 25, 2004, Andrew Veniamin, Williams' right-hand man, was shot and killed at a restaurant following an argument with a former associate. Days later, on March 31, 2004, **Lewis**

Moran, patriarch of the Moran family, was shot to death while he was in a club. Williams pleaded guilty to his murder.

Arrest & Imprisonment

On October 29, 2004, William was convicted of drug trafficking and sentenced to seven years in prison. Years later, he confessed to his part in the Melbourne Gangland Killings.

Trial

In a Victoria court, Carl Williams pleaded guilty to the murders of Lewis Moran, Jason Moran, and Mark Mallia. Williams also admitted that he had conspired to murder gangland rival Mario Condello. As part of a plea deal with the police, Williams was not charged for his involvement in the planning of Mark Moran's murder, who was Jason Moran's half-brother. Additionally, it was revealed that Williams was serving a twenty-one-year sentence for the 2003 murder of Michael Marshall, a detail that had previously been suppressed.

On July 19, 2006, Williams was sentenced to 27 years imprisonment with a 21-year non-parole period for the murder of Michael Marshall. Later, on May 7, 2007, he received multiple sentences for his involvement in the gangland killings:

• Life imprisonment for the murders of Jason Moran and Mark Mallia.

• 25 years imprisonment for the murder of Lewis Moran.

• 25 years imprisonment for conspiring to murder Mario Condello.

Family Affairs

In November 2007, his father was sentenced to more than four years for drug trafficking, and on November 22, 2008, his mother, Barbara Williams, was found dead in her Melbourne home from an overdose of unspecified drugs. It was alleged to be an act of suicide. She had been suffering from depression. Carl was in prison at the time, and he was refused leave to attend her funeral.

On April 19, 2010, the Herald Sun Newspaper reported that the Victoria Police paid $8,000 in school fees for Carl Williams' daughter, Dakota. The reason for the payment was not initially disclosed. However, during Williams' 2011 murder trial, testimony revealed that he had become a police informant and had struck a deal with the Assistant Commissioner. It was believed that Victoria Police covered Dhakota's private school fees in exchange for Williams' cooperation as an informant while in prison.

The unusual arrangement between Victoria Police and Williams' family brought significant public attention to Dhakota.

Dhakota Williams, the daughter of Carl Williams, has become a notable public figure in Australia. Often described in the media as a "gangland heiress," Dhakota's personal life has been a frequent topic of news headlines in recent years. Besides the police paying for her private school fees, in late 2022, Dhakota captured public attention by joining the adult website *OnlyFans*, bringing her back into the media spotlight.

Death

On April 19, 2010, Carl Williams died in Barwon Prison after another prisoner, Matthew Johnson, bludgeoned him to death with an exercise bike handle. Johnson was later convicted of Williams' murder in December 2011 and received a thirty-two-year sentence in prison.

Williams' funeral took place on April 30,

2010, at St Therese's Catholic Church in Essendon, where he was buried in a golden coffin. By January 2011, it was reported that his grave remained a nameless plot without a headstone.

The Victorian Ombudsman investigated the circumstances of Williams' death, and a report critical of Corrections Victoria was released in April 2012. It highlighted the poor decision to approve Williams sharing a cell with Johnson. The Department of Justice Secretary Penny Armytage and Corrections Victoria Commissioner Bob Hastings resigned after its release.

In 2019, during the Royal Commission into the Management of Police Informants, former Deputy Commissioner (Crime) for Victoria Police, Sir Kenneth Lloyd Jones, submitted a statement expressing his belief that prison staff were involved in Williams' death.

NINETEEN

Christopher Worrell & James Miller

THE TRURO MURDERS

"The Truro Murders" refers to a series of killings east of the town of Truro in South Australia. The remains of a young woman and a teenage girl were discovered in the bushland in 1978 and 1979, respectively. The discovery unearthed a killer's dumping site.

When the police searched nearby areas, further findings were made. In all, the remains of seven women and girls were found: five in Truro, one in Wingfield, and one in Port Gawler. It was determined the victims had been murdered over two months between 1976 and 1977.

Discovery of The Truro Murders

On April 20, 1978, while mushroom hunting in the forest area near Truro, William (Bill) Thomas and his brother stumbled upon what they initially believed to be a cow's leg bone. Bill's wife, Valda, had concerns about the find and convinced her husband to revisit the site two days later.

Upon closer inspection, they discovered that the bone had a shoe attached, and inside the shoe was human skin and painted toenails. Clothes, blood stains, and additional bones were found nearby.

The remains were later identified as Veronica Knight, an eighteen-year-old woman who had disappeared from an Adelaide street two days before Christmas in 1976. The lack of an apparent cause of death and the remote location led authorities to initially believe that Veronica might have gotten lost and died of thirst. Her death was not considered suspicious.

Almost a year later, on April 15, 1979, police found the remains of sixteen-year-old Sylvia Pittmann about 2 km from where Veronica's remains had been located. Syliva had vanished around the same time as Veronica.

Police linked the bodies of the two dead women found close to each other with five other women who had been reported missing by their families. Eleven days later, an extensive search party found the remains of two more victims, Connie Lordanides and Vicki Howell, on the opposite side of Swamp Road. They were confirmed to be two of the five missing women.

Perpetrators

Two men are believed to have committed the murders: twenty-three-year-old Christopher Worrell and thirty-eight-year-old James Miller.

Worrell was described as young and charismatic but a sociopath. Miller was a drifter who worked as a laborer. He was Worrell's homosexual partner for a time.

The two men met while they were both in prison. Worrell had been convicted of rape, while

Miller was caught burglarizing a house. During their time in prison, the two became sexually involved. Worrell was the dominant partner, telling Miller what to do and when. After their release, they decided to live together and continue this relationship.

Worrell often told Miller to perform sexual acts on him while he read pornographic, predominantly BDSM, magazines.

Worrell actually preferred women, so this element of their relationship later ceased, and they became more like brothers.

Later, a terrifying pattern for the duo was revealed during the trial. Worrell and Miller would drive around at night in Worrell's 1969 Chrysler Valiant wagon on the lookout for any women that Worrell might be able to pick up and maybe have sex with. Worrell was good-looking and usually had no problems picking up women and convincing them to have sex.

Once they had found a woman who would get in the car with them, Miller would drive them to a quiet, isolated area in a park or something like that. Once parked, Miller would leave the car and let Worrell and the woman be alone. Usually, Worrell would tie up the woman before having sex with her. After they were done, Miller would drive them back to town and drop her off.

Miller described later how these "pick-ups" became increasingly terrifying. Worrell sometimes raped the women who refused his advances. As the violence escalated, he eventually began murdering them. Miller claimed he was unaware that murder would occur beforehand, stating that it only happened sometimes and not others. As Worrell started to commit murder, Miller became more and more frightened of him.

The murders ended on February 19, 1977, when Worrell and a woman he had abducted, Deborah Skuse, were killed in a car crash. Miller survived the accident but suffered from depression and became homeless after Worrell's death. His fragile state of mind and a chance comment eventually led to a breakthrough in the case.

Arrest

Worrell's girlfriend, Amelia, told Miller at Worrell's funeral that he had mentioned he thought he had a blood clot in his brain. The discussion prompted Miller to open up to Amelia, revealing Worrell's fascination with thrill killing.

He even suggested that the clot might have been the cause of Worrell's violent behavior.

In May 1979, Amelia provided this information to the police, leading to Miller's arrest. It also led to the subsequent collection of a $30,000 reward for Amelia. She claimed she had not come forward earlier because she had no proof of the admission. She also saw little point in going to the police as Worrell was already dead. But after reading about the murders in the newspaper, she decided to tell what she knew. Without her information, the murders might have never been solved.

Miller was arrested and brought in for questioning by the police. Initially, he denied knowing anything, but eventually, he admitted that Amelia had "done what I should have." He told detectives about three more bodies and showed the police where the bodies were dumped in Truro.

Miller initially admitted to six of the assaults and murders but later recanted, realizing his honesty was self-incriminating. He continued to visit the graves of Skuse and Worrell, placing a memorial notice in the *Adelaide Advertiser* one year after their deaths, expressing his hope of meeting them again in the afterlife.

Victims

Eighteen-year-old **Veronica Knight** was separated from her friend while shopping and accepted a ride home from Christopher Worrell and James Miller on December 23, 1976. They convinced her to go for a drive in the Adelaide foothills. While Miller went for a walk, Worrell killed her. Miller claimed he angrily confronted Worrell, who then threatened him with a knife. They dumped Veronica's body at Truro and returned to work the following day.

Worrell and Miller picked up fifteen-year-old **Tania Kenny** on January 2, 1977, when she was hitchhiking from Victor Harbor. They drove to Miller's sister's home, where Worrell killed her. Miller claimed Worrell threatened to kill him if he did not help. They buried Tania at Wingfield that night.

Worrell offered sixteen-year-old **Juliet Mykyta** a lift home on January 21, 1977, while she was waiting at a bus stop. Instead of bringing her home, they drove her to Port Wakefield. Miller was present when Worrell tied her up and later strangled her. Juliet's remains were found at Truro.

Worrell and Miller picked up sixteen-year-old **Sylvia Pittmann** on February 6, 1977, while she was waiting for a train at the Adelaide Railway Station. Her body was disposed of at Truro after Miller returned from a walk.

Twenty-six-year-old **Vickie Howell** was with Worrell when Miller arrived to pick him up at a post office on February 7, 1977. Miller went for a walk and returned to find her dead. They took her body to Truro.

Worrell and Miller picked up sixteen-year-old **Connie Iordanides** on February 9, 1977, but she became frightened when they drove in the wrong direction of where she said she needed to go. Miller stopped at Wingfield, where Worrell forced her into the back seat. They later went to Truro to dump her body.

Twenty-year-old **Deborah Lamb** was hitchhiking on West Terrace on February 12, 1977, when the duo picked her up. They drove to Port Gawler, where Worrell buried her alive after Miller took a walk.

Deborah Skuse was killed in a car crash that also claimed Worrell's life on February 19, 1977. Deborah, a friend's ex-girlfriend, had accompanied them to Mount Gambier. Worrell was driving when the car blew a tire and rolled, killing both Worrell and Skuse and breaking Miller's shoulderblade.

All the victims had been strangled before they were buried, except for Lamb, who was buried alive. Criminologist Paul Wilson suggested that if

Worrell had not died, the Truro murders could have escalated into a much more devastating killing spree as the time between the murders was getting shorter.

Trial

James Miller was charged and tried for seven murders. Legally, Miller argued that he never directly engaged in any murders, nor did he explicitly agree to support Worrell in the murders. Nonetheless, he was found guilty of murder because he was considered to have been a part of the murders. Miller was at the crime scene when the murders happened, and even though he never took part in the killing of the victim, he knew the murder was happening and did nothing to stop it. And afterward, he helped to get rid of the bodies.

Miller was found guilty of six of the murders in March 1980, but he was acquitted of the Veronica Knight murder. He received six life terms in prison to be served consecutively.

In 1999, Miller applied for a non-parole period under new laws, and on February 8, 2000, the court permitted him to apply for parole in 2014 after serving thirty-five years in prison.

Death

On October 21, 2008, James Miller, then sixty-eight years old, died of liver failure, a complication of having hepatitis C. He also had prostate and lung cancer. At the time of his death, Miller was one of the longest-serving prisoners in the state.

TWENTY

John and Sarah Makin

THE HATPIN MURDERS

John Sidney Makin and Sarah Jane Makin were Australian "baby farmers" convicted in New South Wales in 1892. The couple responded to a series of advertisements from unmarried mothers seeking adoption or childcare services for their babies, accepting the infants' care in exchange for a "premium" payment. In the month from October 12th to November 12th, 1892, the remains of fifteen infants were found buried in different yards of the houses where the Makins had lived.

In March 1893, the couple were tried for murder and found guilty, resulting in both being sentenced to death. However, Sarah Makin's sentence was later commuted to life imprisonment. John Makin was hanged on August 15, 1893, while Sarah Makin served her sentence, and after eighteen and a half years, was released in April 1911 following a petition for her early release by her daughters.

Background

John Sidney Makin was born on February 14, 1845, in Dapto, near Wollongong, to William Makin, a convict, and his wife Ellen Bolton. He was the fourth of eleven children born to the couple. Sarah Jane Sutcliffe was born on December 20, 1845, in Sussex Street, Sydney, to Emanuel Sutcliffe, a mill worker and former convict, and Ellen Murphy. Sarah's first marriage was to a mariner, Charles Edwards, in Sydney on April 29, 1865. She then married John Makin on August 27, 1871.

John and Sarah Makin had at least ten children: five sons and five daughters. The daughters reportedly involved in their baby farming operation were Blanche, Florence, Clarice, and Daisy. Sarah's daughter from her first marriage, Minnie, was married and estranged from the family. At the time of their arrest, their sons, except for the youngest, Thomas, Clarice, and Daisy, were all living elsewhere.

Around 1881, John Makin was employed as a drayman for a brewer. In November of that year, he was convicted of stealing and imprisoned for three months. By 1885, Makin was working as a green grocer's van driver. But in May 1886, while he was driving for work, he ran over a four-year-old child crossing Elizabeth Street, causing the child to suffer a concussion and be hospitalized.

After John was injured in another accident, the couple turned to "baby farming" as a source of income, taking on the care of illegitimate babies in exchange for payment. John was described as "by no means an industrious man," having "not done much work" in the three or four years before November 1892. His last known employment was with Mr. R. Bedford, a livery-stable proprietor and main contractor. Bedford employed him as a driver in November

1891, but John left suddenly after about six weeks.

During the first few months of 1891, while living on Levey Street in Chippendale, John Makin did no work and was often seen idling about in front of the house. His neighbors reported that John boasted about having private means. He claimed he received one pound a week from a Wollongong property inherited from his mother, who died in 1890. Despite his bragging, his neighbors reported that the family always seemed miserably poor.

First Discoveries

On October 11, 1892, James Mahoney and Frank Cooney dug a trench in the backyard of 25 Burren Street, Macdonaldtown, to connect a service pipe from the house to the sewer. Mahoney initially found the "very much decomposed" remains of what he thought was a cat buried under six inches of earth. The following morning, Mahoney discovered the body of a female infant buried about a foot deep, around 30 yards from the remains he had found the previous day. They called the police.

The Newtown police described the bodies as

being "very much decomposed" and appeared to have been buried for several months. The remains were removed to the South Sydney Morgue. At the morgue, it was revealed that the remains were those of a male and a female infant, both buried with clothing. It was initially estimated that the female had been buried for about six weeks and the male for about three months.

Suspicion instantly went to whoever the property's tenants were at that time. Detectives traced the previous tenants to John and Sarah Makin using tenancy records. Once they had their names, they could see how often the Makin family moved in recent years, which they found suspicious. They decided to look at the other properties where the couple had lived in recent years.

A few days later, on October 14th, they found another body in nearby Redfern on Zamia Street. The decomposed body of a male infant, estimated to be about 20 days old, was found in a vacant lot.

On another Redfern property where the family once lived, 6 Wells Street, Senior Constable Joyce noticed some recently disturbed ground. Digging at the spot, he found it empty. He concluded that the body on Zamia Street had been recently moved there. And that it had come from the Wells Street property. The body was too decomposed to determine the cause of death or even if the child had been born alive.

An inquest was ordered to find out the identity of the two babies and how they died. On October 26, 1892, before the coroner and a jury, testimonies were given by the two workers who discovered the bodies, the doctors who performed autopsies, the Government analyst, Senior Constable Joyce, several members of the Makin family, and several neighbors.

Medical evidence determined that one of the infants was female and one was male. The female infant had been stillborn, while the male baby, aged five to eight months, had been dead for three to six months. On the final day of the inquest on October 28th, Blanche, Florence, John, and Sarah Makin testified. Sarah claimed that a day after moving into the Macdonaldtown house in late June, she took in a two-week-old female child to wet nurse, being paid ten shillings a week. She claimed that in mid-August, "the mother took it away and said she was going to Melbourne." Sarah also claimed this child "was the first and only one" she had taken in. John corroborated his wife's testimony.

The city coroner, John Woore, told the jury

that the case was "surrounded by suspicion" and that the bodies had undoubtedly been placed there secretly. However, after a few minutes of deliberation, the jury returned an open verdict. They were unable to determine either the identities of the children or how they died. So they could not say that it was murder. Without more information, the Makins were only guilty of not officially reporting the death of the children.

Further Investigation

The police decided to keep looking around. For one, the Makin family had lived in eleven residences since 1890. They also knew that Sarah Makin lied at the inquest. She denied being a midwife or having any other children but had advertised her services. They also found it suspicious that shortly after they visited the family at Wells St. in Redfern after the discovery of the two infant bodies, they quickly packed up and moved again to Chippendale.

On November 2nd, Senior Constable James Joyce and Constable Alexander Brown, plain-clothes officers from the Newtown Police Station, went to the house on Burren Street and began digging in the yard. They discovered the bodies of an additional five babies.

The following afternoon, on November 3rd, Joyce arrested John Makin and his daughters, Blanche and Florence, at their house in Chippendale and took them to Newtown Police Station. Sarah Makin had already been arrested earlier at Parramatta and was at the station.

During questioning, Blanche revealed that she remembered her mother had cared for three infants at one time. When Blanche was asked why she didn't say this at the inquest, she said it was because her parents had told her to claim she knew nothing about any other children in the house.

John and Sarah were charged on suspicion of causing the death of a female child. Blanche and Florence Makin were also charged. The Makins' youngest child, two-year-old Cecil, was taken under the care of a neighbor.

The police announced the arrests and their intention to continue their investigation. They would dig up all the yards where the family lived over the past three or four years, as Senior Constable Joyce believed the Makins had been "engaged in baby farming" during this period. By mid-November, yards on Botany, East, and Kettle streets had been searched, but no discoveries were made. Further searches were planned for Bullanaming Street, St. Peters, and Howard Street.

More Discoveries

Between October 12th and November 12th, police discovered the remains of fifteen infants buried on the premises where the Makins had lived. The discoveries went like so:

At **25 Burren Street, Macdonaldtown**, where the Makin family resided from June 29th to August 16, 1892, the bodies of seven infants were recovered from the yard. Two were found on October 11th and 12th, and another five in early November 1892.

The first body was a male infant, aged from five to eight months, buried for three to six months. The second was a stillborn female infant.

The third was a male infant, aged from two to three months, buried for four to six months. The fourth was ultimately determined to be the female child of Minnie Davis and Horace Bothamley. The fifth was a female infant, estimated to be about ten days old, buried for about three months.

In a vacant lot on **Zamia Street, Redfern**, one body was found on October 14, 1892. It was believed to have been disinterred from the Makins' backyard at Wells Street after they learned of the discoveries in Macdonaldtown.

At **109 George Street, Redfern**, four infants' bodies were found on November 9, 1892. They were designated "A," "B," "C," and "D." The body marked "D" was later identified as Horace Amber Murray, for whose murder the Makins were later charged. The Makin family rented 109 George Street, using the surname "Mason," from May 21st until June 27th, 1892.

At **11 Alderson Street, Redfern**, one infant body was found in the yard on November 11, 1892, designated "E." The infant was wrapped in black cloth and buried at a depth of two feet. The estimated age at death was two to six weeks, and the burial period was six to twelve months. The gender was impossible to ascertain at the time. An inquiry held on December 14, 1892, returned an open verdict with no evidence as to the cause of death. The Makin family rented the house from December 7, 1891, to January 28, 1892.

At **28 Levey Street, Chippendale**, next door to the Appin Hotel, police found the remains of two infants on November 12, 1892. The bodies were buried together near the kitchen wall, with little remaining but the bones. The Makin family had occupied this house in November 1891 for six or seven weeks.

Baby Farming Activities

As a result of the examinations by the City Coroner, only two of the fifteen infants could be identified: **Minnie Davis**, the female child of

Minnie Davis and Horace Bothamley, and **Horace Murray**, the baby boy of Amber Murray. John and Sarah Makin were charged with causing their deaths, and a trial was set.

Some of the Makins' baby-farming activities came to light at the inquests held in the Coroner's Court and the subsequent trial. Some of the infants found may have been from these activities:

On February 12, 1892, nineteen-year-old **Agnes Ward**, a domestic servant living at Cook's River, gave birth to a male child at the residence of Mrs. Elizabeth Terry, a midwife, in Summer Hill. The birth was registered in Ashfield, and the child was named **Charles**. On April 27th, Agnes placed an advertisement in the *Evening News* seeking a "kind lady" to adopt her baby boy.

The next day, John, Sarah Makin, and their daughter Daisy met with Agnes at Mrs. Terry's residence. They agreed to adopt the infant for £5 and promised to be very kind to him. John Makin claimed he was taking the child to fill the gap left by the death of his child named "Johnny" and that this child would take the deceased child's place. He mentioned that they were living in Kettle Street in Redfern but would soon move to take over a 'piggery.' He promised to send their new address so Agnes could visit the boy. One of the bodies found buried at 109 George Street was provisionally identified as Agnes Ward's male child.

At the Benevolent Asylum, **Clara Risby**, a domestic servant from Woolloomooloo, had a baby girl on April 15, 1892. On May 4th, she placed an advertisement in the *Evening News* seeking a "kind person" to adopt her baby girl for life, offering a premium of £5.

Using the surname "McLachlan," the Makins responded to the ad from their 16 East Street, Redfern residence. Clara and her married step-sister, Mary Sargent, took the baby girl to the Makin's house on May 16th, where she was handed over. Sarah Makin promised to raise the girl as her own, while John Makin claimed they planned to take a poultry farm at Rockdale. Clara visited her baby girl on May 18th, but on a subsequent visit, she was told that "Mrs. McLachlan" was out with the child. When she tried visiting again on May 24th, she found the house empty.

Mary Stacey, a domestic servant from Petersham, gave birth to a baby girl on April 17, 1892. On June 17th, she advertised for someone to adopt her child and received a letter from the Makins, who used the surname "Ray." They offered to take charge of the child for a payment of £3. Mary visited the family at 109 George Street, where the Makins professed to really like the baby. Sarah agreed to adopt the baby for a payment of £2. Mary handed over her baby girl to Blanche and Clarice Makin when they visited her Petersham residence on June 23rd. A few days later, John and Blanche visited her with the little girl and informed her that they were moving to Hurstville. Mary later visited the home on George Street, which was empty, and then spent two days searching Hurstville for the family, but without success. She then informed the police that the "Ray" family had disappeared with her child.

A domestic servant, **Agnes Todd**, gave birth to a baby girl named **Elsie** around December 1891. From about March 1892, the child was cared for by Maria Sutherland, a married woman living in Alexandria. In June 1892, Agnes paid John Makin £3 to take the child, who he collected from Mrs. Sutherland on June 28th while the Makins lived at 109 George Street. John assured Agnes that he would be an excellent father to the child.

On May 30, 1892, eighteen-year-old **Amber Murray** gave birth to a baby boy named **Horace**. On June 24th, she placed an advertisement in the *Sydney Morning Herald* seeking a "motherly person" to adopt her baby boy, offering to pay a small premium. The same day the ad appeared, a letter was written by either John or Sarah Makin from their George Street address, expressing their willingness to adopt the child for a fee of about £2 10s or £3, and promising to give him "a mother's love and attention." The letter, signed "E. Hill," invited the advertiser to visit the address if the proposal suited her.

Soon afterward, Amber took the child to the

Redfern address. When the Makins saw the child, they told Amber he was the kind they would like to have, "as they had lost a little boy of their own." She was devastated to have to give him up but handed him over with the payment of £3 and the papers concerning the adoption. Initially, John claimed he did not understand the papers, but then read through and signed them, first as "John Leslie," which he scratched out and signed as "Hill." As Amber left, Horace was brought out for her to see one last time. The Makins relocated to Burren Street in Macdonaldtown within a day or two after that, and she didn't see her baby again.

On June 10, 1892, **Mignonette "Minnie" Davis**, a domestic servant in Paddington, gave birth to a baby girl named after herself. The birth was registered in Newtown, and the father's details were included. On June 21st, Minnie Davis placed an advertisement in the *Sydney Morning Herald* seeking a "kind person" to care for their child until they could resolve their affairs.

Using the surname "Bert," John Makin responded to the ad. Minnie and the child's father, Horace Bothamley, visited the Makin's house on

George Street the following day. John agreed to take the baby and care for her for ten shillings a week and assured the parents they could see baby Minnie whenever they liked. They left the baby and some infant clothing with the Makins.

Minnie returned two days later to see her child and brought more clothing, with Sarah present. However, when Minnie and Horace next visited, they discovered that the Makins had moved.

After locating their new address on Burren Street, Minnie and Horace visited a week later. They saw the baby and paid their ten shillings. The couple started visiting every Saturday to see Baby Minnie and paying the Makins their weekly fee. During one visit, Minnie and Horace discovered the Makin's real surname when they saw a card reading "Mrs. Makin, ladies nurse and qualified midwife." Sarah admitted to deceiving them.

On July 23rd, they were informed that the baby had a cold. The following Saturday, she was very ill, and John told them he would take her to the doctor on Monday. A few days after that, John sent Horace a telegram informing him that the child had died.

On Thursday, August 4th, Minnie and Horace arrived at the Macdonaldtown residence with flowers to view the baby's body. The deceased child was laid out on a board, "enshrouded in a long white gown." John told Minnie, "Perhaps it's better that it did die." When asked about the cause of death, John replied, "It wasted away. I will not bother to get a certificate from the doctor." He claimed that a coffin had been ordered and that he would bury the infant for two pounds. The Makins did not attend the funeral.

Trial

On Monday, March 6, 1893, John and Sarah Makin went to trial in the Central Criminal Court before Justice Stephen. They were charged with the "felonious and malicious" murder of Horace Amber Murray on June 29, 1892, at Redfern. They also faced a charge of murdering "a certain male infant whose name is unknown" on the same day and at the same place. The second count referred to the same child as a contingency against any technicality concerning the child's identity. The Makins pleaded not guilty and were defended by Thomas Williamson.

During the Crown Prosecutor Patrick Healy's address and the witnesses' testimonies, John Makin sat in the dock with his legs and arms crossed while his wife hid her face with a handkerchief.

Among the witnesses was Amber Murray, who detailed the events leading to her handing over her infant son to the Makins. She identified the clothes found on the remains of the child discovered under the window of 109 George Street, Redfern, as those that her son was wearing when she handed him over. She had made the gown herself, and the shirt was identified as a gift a friend gave her for the baby.

It was not established how the babies died. Many of the bodies were too decomposed by the time they were discovered, but Constable James Joyce gave evidence of finding bloodstains on the infant's clothing, just under the armpits, and believed the infants had been stabbed in the heart with a hatpin.

The Makins' own daughters testified against them in court. Sixteen-year-old Clarice stated that she recognized clothing recovered from one of the dead babies that was previously in the custody of her mother. At the inquest on December 16, 1892, Clarice Makin testified that they took six babies with them when the family moved from George Street in Redfern to Burren Street in Macdonaldtown – two were in a cradle, two were in a perambulator, her mother carried one, and Daisy carried another. But at the trial, Clarice claimed no recollection of seeing six babies being taken to Burren Street. Eleven-year-old Daisy recalled that two young girls that followed them to Macdonaldtown, but not Horace.

On the second day of the trial, Edward Jordan, a horse trainer who had been locked up in Newtown police station with John Makin, testified that Makin had told him about the seven babies that had been found, mentioning an eighth that had not yet been discovered. Makin reportedly said that when the eighth was found, "he would never see daylight anymore—that was what a man got for obliging people." Jordan also claimed Makin had boasted that "no doctor could prove that he had poisoned any of the children because he never went near a chemist."

The Crown's case was completed early on March 8th, the third day of the trial.

The defense attorney, Williamson, did not call either Makin family member to the stand, nor did they call any evidence. When it was his time to address the jury, he argued that the Crown had failed to prove a murder had been committed and that the cause of death for any of the infants had not been determined. He claimed it was "an insult to their intelligence" to ask the jury to conclude that the child in question had been murdered simply because other children were found dead.

In Healy's statement, the Crown Prosecutor acknowledged the extraordinary and unique nature of the case but believed the jury would have no difficulty concluding that the child had been murdered.

The jury retired at five in the afternoon to consider their verdict. At around nine o'clock, after discussions between the jury foreman and the judge, it was determined that the jury was unlikely to reach a verdict that night, and they were sequestered for the rest of the night.

When the jury returned to the court at 10 a.m. the next day, March 9th, the foreman announced a verdict of guilty of the murder of Horace Murray for both John and Sarah Makin. However, the foreman added a strong recommendation for mercy for Sarah Makin.

Justice Stephen deferred passing his sentence pending a determination by the Full Court of the Supreme Court on points regarding the admissibility of specific evidence at the trial raised by defense attorney Williamson.

First Appeal

The appeal against the conviction of John and Sarah Makin was heard on March 23rd before the Full Bench of the Supreme Court, which included Justice Windeyer, Justice Innes, and Justice Foster. Sir Julian Salomons, Queen's Counsel, led the support for the appeal, while Francis Rogers, Q.C., headed the team supporting the conviction. The grounds for the appeal were:

1. That Justice Stephen was wrong in admitting evidence of the discovery of other bodies besides the one alleged to be Horace Murray,
2. That the judge erred in admitting the testimony of mothers (apart from Amber Murray) who had given up their children to the Makins,
3. That there was no evidence to prove the body marked 'D' was that of Horace Murray,
4. That there was no evidence of the death or cause of death of Horace Murray or that he had been murdered.

After hearing the arguments, the Full Bench advised they would consider their decision.

The appeal judges took a week to deliberate. Their decision was delivered on March 30th, dismissing the appeal and confirming the convictions. The leading judgment, twenty-seven pages in length, was written by Justice Windeyer and concurred with by Justice Foster. Justice Innes disagreed with Windeyer's reasoning for admitting evidence of the deaths of the other babies. Nevertheless, he concurred with his fellow judges that the convictions against the Makins should stand.

Sentencing

On the same day their appeal was dismissed, John and Sarah Makin appeared in the Central Criminal Court for sentencing by Justice Stephen. John Makin stood in the dock with a semi-defiant attitude, which he maintained until the end. Sarah Makin was assisted to her place and hid her face in a handkerchief throughout her time in court. Their solicitor indicated that they planned to appeal to the British Privy Council.

As he passed the sentence, Justice Stephen recounted how the Makins had taken money from

Horace Murray's mother, misleading her with promises they never intended to fulfill. He noted that they had already determined the child's death, misled the mother with false names, and deceived her about their address. He also compared the burial of the child in their yard "as you would the carcass of a dog."

Justice Stephen condemned the Makins for engaging in the worst phase of baby farming, marked by its most hideous and revolting aspects. He declared that the "ghastly evidence" from the yards where they had lived testified to their "nefarious and hellish trade," destroying infants' lives for gain.

After his address, the judge sentenced both Makins to execution by hanging. In Sarah Makin's case, he added that he would forward a recommendation of mercy to the Executive. Towards the end of the sentencing, Sarah Makin collapsed and had to be carried from the court by two constables as she cried out, "Oh! My babies. Oh! my babies."

Second Appeal

To send an appeal to the Privy Council in Britain, the consent of the New South Wales Government was needed. A petition seeking this consent was sent to the Executive Council on April 11, 1893. On the same day, the Council commuted Sarah Makin's death sentence to life imprisonment. Later, on April 21st, the Council postponed John Makin's execution for three months to allow for the appeal to the Privy Council.

When the Makins' petition was received in London, the seven Law Lords of the Judicial Committee of the Privy Council reviewed the case. Their verdict, sent by cable to the New South Wales Government on July 21st, informed that the appeal was dismissed. However, they reserved their reasons for the dismissal until the following November. The notification of the Privy Council's dismissal of the appeal allowed the New South Wales Attorney-General to resume the judicial process and set the date for John Makin's execution.

Final Plea for Mercy

In early August 1893, John Makin wrote to Premier Sir Henry Parkes, highlighting what he considered weak points in the evidence and requesting a reprieve from the death sentence. The communication was forwarded to the

Minister for Justice, who found nothing in the letter that would prompt the Government to reconsider the sentence. However, Parkes agreed to meet with a Makin family delegation in Wollongong.

On August 11th, two of Makin's brothers, his sister-in-law and members of parliament for Illawarra, Archibald Campbell and John Nicholson, met with the Colonial Secretary, Sir George Dibbs. They presented a petition signed by several citizens of Wollongong. The family delegation did not attempt to delve into the merits of the case but requested that, for the sake of Makin's brothers, their families, and his own family, his punishment be commuted to match that of his wife's life sentence.

During the meeting, the Makin family and their representatives argued that John had been led astray by his wife, Sarah, whom they described as "the arch-aggressor" and "the arch-fiend" in the matter. Sarah Makin was portrayed as a "terrible woman" with a temper more akin to a fiend than a woman. Dibbs reminded the family that unless new pertinent facts were brought forward, the Government had no power to intervene in the legal process. However, he promised to call a meeting of the Executive

Council the following Monday to discuss the matter.

As expected, the Executive Council was unconvinced by the petition to save John Makin's life and decided that "the law should take its course."

Justice

John Makin was executed by hanging just after 9 a.m. on Tuesday, August 15, 1893, on the gallows within the precincts of Darlinghurst Gaol. It was reported that the condemned man "appeared resigned to his fate," having placed little hope in the appeals for a reprieve. Makin had met with his wife the previous Thursday before she was taken to Bathurst Gaol. On the same day, he was visited by his daughters Blanche and Florence, his brothers Daniel and Joseph, and his stepdaughter Minnie Helbi.

Makin left two written statements, one denying his guilt and the other addressed to his children, which was "couched in very affectionate terms."

The official report stated that the execution "was properly conducted."

On August 10, 1893, five days before her husband's execution, Sarah Makin was transferred from Darlinghurst Gaol to Bathurst Gaol. In May 1895, she was moved back to Darlinghurst Gaol and returned to Bathurst in November 1898. During her second stint at Bathurst, she was given a job as a hospital attendant at the jail.

Sarah Makin's health deteriorated during her incarceration, and she occasionally suffered from intestinal hemorrhages. By 1907, two of Sarah's daughters, Florence (then married and known as Florence Anderson) and Minnie Helbi, were sufficiently concerned about their mother's health that they each wrote to the Attorney-General requesting her release from prison. However, their pleas were refused.

In August 1909, Sarah Makin was transferred to the newly constructed State Reformatory for Women at Long Bay Gaol.

In 1911, with a new Attorney-General in office, Makin and her family began another campaign for her release so that she could spend her last days with her family. This time, the Government, considering her advanced age and declining health, recommended her release. Sarah

Makin was discharged quietly and anonymously from Long Bay Gaol on April 29, 1911, into the care of Florence Anderson and her husband.

A few months after her release, Sarah moved to Belgrave Street in Petersham to live with her eldest daughter, Minnie Helby (formerly spelled Helbi), who was suffering from bowel cancer and died in February 1912. Sarah Makin remained in the house at Petersham with her son-in-law, Carl Helby. As her health began to deteriorate, Florence and her husband moved in.

Sarah Makin died on September 13, 1918, aged seventy-two years, from senile decay and heart failure, possibly due to tertiary syphilis. She was buried in Rookwood Cemetery.

Aftermath

New South Wales had a Children's Protection Act in place before the Makins' baby-farming activities were discovered. It was enacted on March 31, 1892. The Act aimed to regulate individuals who took children into their care. It required a written order by a Justice of the Peace for anyone taking a child under three years of age for payment, and it regulated the payments so that they could not be more than twenty shillings. It also included registration to be able to do it. Additionally, the Act banned the payment of 'premiums' to baby farmers. Despite these measures, the legislation proved ineffective in preventing the kinds of abuses the Makin case revealed.

At the time, it was possible that the Makins' could have legally gotten away with it. At the time, no legal principle existed that allowed evidence of other criminal misconduct to be brought into a trial. Justice Stephen permitted evidence of the other bodies, in addition to Horace Murray, just because it made "common sense" to do so. After the Privy Council confirmed the March 1893 appeal decision, the principle that "evidence of a defendant's other criminal misconduct could be relevant" was incorporated into British common law.

Sources

1. https://www.theage.com.au/national/call-for-second-life-term-for-murderer-dupas-20040813-gdyg50.html
2. https://web.archive.org/web/20071206082302/http://www.abc.net.au/news/newsitems/200609/s1739188.htm
3. https://www.theage.com.au/national/a-tragic-life-ends-at-the-hands-of-a-monster-20040812-gdyfvy.html
4. https://www.theage.com.au/national/body-looked-like-mannequin-20040729-gdycmt.html
5. https://www.theage.com.au/national/1m-reward-to-find-halvagis-killer-20050201-gdzh5z.html
6. https://www.theage.com.au/national/court-told-to-speed-up-murder-trial-20061115-gdotsv.html
7. https://web.archive.org/web/20090714084032/
8. http://www.theage.com.au/news/national/fraser-seeks-1m-reward/2007/08/10/1186530579946.html
9. https://archive.ph/20121230141859/
10. http://www.news.com.au/story/0,27574,26208728-29277,00.html#selection-245.0-3529.18
11. https://www.news.com.au/national/peter-dupas-found-guilty-of-murder-of-mersina-

halvagis-for-second-time/story-e6frfkvr-1225956603651

12. https://www.theage.com.au/national/stop-pandering-to-sicko-says-doyle-20040629-gdy4tg.html

13. https://web.archive.org/web/20120709001907/

14. http://aussiecriminals.com.au/high-profile-criminals/paul-charles-denyer-the-frankston-serial-killer/

15. https://www.abc.net.au/news/2023-05-10/frankston-serial-killer-paul-denyer-denied-parole/102208802

16. https://www.newspapers.com/newspage/123020445/

17. https://www.mamamia.com.au/frankston-murders-paul-denyer/

18. https://www.theage.com.au/national/victoria/frankston-serial-killer-paul-denyer-to-stay-behind-bars-20230510-p5d7ce.html

19. https://media.heraldsun.com.au/multimedia/2013/april/denyerletters/index03.html

20. https://web.archive.org/web/20080602094844/

21. http://www.abc.net.au/7.30/content/2003/s1023113.htm

22. https://www.heraldsun.com.au/leader/inner-south/parents-of-murdered-teen-natalie-russell-thank-community-20-years-on/news-story/40bde1ae9748a388d1a47a018355fe7b

23. https://news.google.com/newspapers?id=G0YVAAAAIBAJ&sjid=rJYDAAAAIBAJ&pg=6986,1244522

24. https://www.couriermail.com.au/news/
    queensland/the-mutilator-dead-at-90-william-
    macdonald-who-cut-off-victims-genitalia-was-
    nsws-longest-serving-prisoner/story-fnmd7bxx-
    1227353530066
25. https://trove.nla.gov.au/newspaper/article/
    109898550
26. https://trove.nla.gov.au/newspaper/article/
    105853099
27. https://australianroyalty.net.au/tree/
    purnellmccord.ged/individual/I55606/Alfred-
    Reginald-Greenfield
28. https://trove.nla.gov.au/newspaper/article/
    131733133
29. https://news.google.com/newspapers?id=
    qH1WAAAAIBAJ&sjid=vOUDAAAAIBAJ&
    pg=6814,6187726
30. https://www.smh.com.au/national/nsw/
    william-the-mutilator-macdonald-nsws-oldest-
    prisoner-dead-at-90-20150512-ggzr52.html
31. https://web.archive.org/web/
    20081123125648/
32. http://www.trutv.com/library/crime/
    serial_killers/partners/birnie/2.html
33. https://www.mamamia.com.au/daughter-of-
    david-birnie/
34. https://www.news.com.au/national/breaking-
    news/serial-killer-birnie-to-remain-in-wa-jail/
    news-story/
    f9836a19a7818d7128298ac8f899104d
35. https://www.perthnow.com.au/news/wa/
    birnie-survivor-kate-moir-and-wa-police-officer-

laura-hancock-together-after-three-decades-ng-902072b9ad2a711520bcdfc83c4e3be7

36. https://www.mamamia.com.au/kate-moir-escape-story/

37. https://thewest.com.au/news/wa/missing-mum-linked-to-birnie-murders-ng-b88374591z

38. https://www.smh.com.au/national/serial-killer-and-torturer-due-for-sentence-review-20100107-lv7u.html

39. https://www.smh.com.au/national/serial-killer-found-hanged-in-cell-20051007-gdm7lb.html

40. https://www.perthnow.com.au/news/wa/evil-serial-killer-david-birnie-was-a-softie-inside---ex-prison-guard-ng-091a0bf60ff3fbdc6
ca96a6c74019a7b

41. https://web.archive.org/web/20030202114507/

42. http://www.postnewspapers.com.au/20030201/news/002.shtml

43. https://web.archive.org/web/20090307082604/

44. http://www.trulyunusual.com/wards/showthread.php?t=3356

45. https://trove.nla.gov.au/work/157756183

46. https://www.heraldsun.com.au/news/law-order/eric-edgar-cooke-the-night-caller-was-one-of-australias-worst-serial-killers-in-1960s-trials/news-story/
137d2aacb035c5aa801f12f7abb8ac66

47. https://web.archive.org/web/20090608200442/

48. http://www.police.wa.gov.au/LinkClick.aspx?

link=PDFs%2FEpisodes_WAPolicingHistory.
pdf&tabid=1060

49. https://www.evidencelockerpodcast.com/
transcripts/transcript-47-the-night-caller-eric-
edgar-cooke-australia

50. https://web.archive.org/web/
20090307124128/

51. http://channelnine.ninemsn.com.au/
crimeinvestigationaustralia/episodes/

52. Blackburn, Estelle 2005 *Broken Lives* Hardie
Grant Books ISBN 9781740640732

53. https://www6.austlii.edu.au/cgi-bin/viewdoc/
au/cases/vic/VSC/2007/220.html

54. https://web.archive.org/web/
20031225055430/

55. http://www.theage.com.au/articles/2003/12/
23/1071941733330.html

56. https://web.archive.org/web/
20050722034456/

57. http://www.theage.com.au/news/national/dna-
tests-link-debs-to-prostitute-death/2005/07/20/
1121539031258.html

58. https://www.watoday.com.au/national/
victoria/debs-tells-court-he-sought-deal-with-
police-over-roberts-evidence-20220505-p5aiou.
html?ref=rss

59. https://www.theage.com.au/national/guilty-of-
killing-two-prostitutes-and-two-policemen-
20111212-1oqzz.html

60. https://www.smh.com.au/national/victim-in-
murder-trial-found-alive-but-three-others-are-
definitely-dead-say-police-20030411-gdgkys.html

61. https://www.couriermail.com.au/news/
    queensland/rockhampton/coroner-to-open-
    fraser-inquest/news-story/
    18e9249673fb2f96d11073e8da8e8a71
62. https://web.archive.org/web/
    20050615215035/
63. http://pansw.org.au/PolNews/Nov38-52.pdf
64. https://web.archive.org/web/
    20090711122538/
65. http://www.citv.com.au/microsite/CrimeInvesti
    gationAustralia/episodes/episode.aspx?id=25
66. https://www.smh.com.au/national/granny-
    killer-found-dead-in-cell-20050910-gdm1ec.html
67. https://www.smh.com.au/national/mystery-
    woman-pays-for-killers-funeral-20050918-
    gdm37w.html
68. https://www.heraldsun.com.au/news/law-
    order/john-wayne-glovers-despicable-urge-to-
    fondle-elderly-women-led-to-at-least-six-vicious-
    murders/story-fni0ffnk-1227517851672?sv=
    46b1d11c0d003ec8477d91b52bea486d
69. https://www.smh.com.au/national/suicide-
    watch-on-sick-granny-killer-20050508-
    gdla1v.html
70. https://trove.nla.gov.au/newspaper/article/
    137171617
71. https://www.smh.com.au/national/nsw/life-
    never-a-picnic-for-the-dirt-poor-troubled-milat-
    clan-20101123-185r8.html
72. https://www.smh.com.au/national/nsw/does-
    crime-run-in-the-milat-family-tree-20101127-
    18bg2.html

73. https://www.smh.com.au/national/milat-case-stalked-by-uncertainty-20050721-gdlq2g.html
74. https://www.biography.com/crime/ivan-milat
75. https://www.smh.com.au/national/friends-born-of-sorrow-20060424-gdnf1a.html?page=fullpage
76. https://www.news.com.au/national/crime/milats-respectful-farewell-that-he-denied-his-victims/news-story/d6fbcf2a85e772a0ad0aaa7e7f441046
77. https://news.google.com/newspapers?nid=1734&dat=19940531&id=MOAhAAAAIBAJ&sjid=1VIEAAAAIBAJ&pg=6928
78. https://www.bbc.com/news/world-australia-48346543
79. https://archive.org/details/evilwithintopmur0000marr
80. https://ses.library.usyd.edu.au/bitstream/handle/2123/8938/Over-our-dead-bodies_Chapman.pdf
81. https://web.archive.org/web/20140110094731/
82. http://www.parliament.nsw.gov.au/prod/parlment/hansart.nsf/V3Key/LA19970520013
83. https://www.theguardian.com/australia-news/2019/oct/27/ivan-milat-chilling-serial-murders-haunt-australia-after-death
84. https://www.smh.com.au/national/murder-tried-and-true-20050211-gdko81.html
85. https://web.archive.org/web/20060312135311/
86. http://www.fireflybooks.com/Publicity/books/4839.html

87. https://trove.nla.gov.au/newspaper/article/231786070

88. https://trove.nla.gov.au/newspaper/article/168972547

89. https://adb.anu.edu.au/biography/leonski-edward-joseph-10814

90. https://trove.nla.gov.au/newspaper/article/203116986

91. https://www.theguardian.com/books/2018/jul/02/the-brownout-strangler-how-a-smiling-psychopath-terrorised-wartime-melbourne

92. https://trove.nla.gov.au/newspaper/article/212094721

93. https://the.honoluluadvertiser.com/article/2001/Apr/22/ln/ln05a.html

94. https://trove.nla.gov.au/newspaper/article/1408956?searchTerm=Arnold+Sodeman

95. https://trove.nla.gov.au/newspaper/article/2407086

96. https://trove.nla.gov.au/newspaper/article/2416859?searchTerm=Arnold+Karl+Sodeman

97. https://www.abc.net.au/news/2013-07-24/derek-percy-linked-to-deaths-of-9-children/4840556

98. https://www.theage.com.au/technology/one-man-so-many-faces-of-evil-20070422-ge4pv0.html

99. https://www.heraldsun.com.au/news/law-order/derek-percy8217s-mother-elaine-admits-she-8216got-rid-of-things8217-as-cops-investigated-child-serial-killings/story-fni0ffnk-1226684583337

100. https://www.nzherald.co.nz/world/derek-percy-believed-to-be-australias-worst-child-serial-killer/EYJIMHUZSYVLQGM4ZGOOQZ5SSA/?c_id=2&objectid=11830363
101. https://www8.austlii.edu.au/cgi-bin/viewdoc/au/cases/nsw/NSWCCA/1999/327.html
102. https://www.newspapers.com/newspage/119690965/
103. https://www.smh.com.au/national/hard-men-turn-to-islam-to-cope-with-jail-20051119-gdmh2o.html
104. https://www.abc.net.au/news/2017-10-30/my-father-is-a-murderer/9066894
105. https://www.youtube.com/watch?v=1nN2TK51Jt0
106. https://www.abc.net.au/news/2019-06-25/alleged-claremont-serial-killer-bradley-edwards-telstra-van/11245168
107. https://www.abc.net.au/news/2019-11-27/claremont-serial-killings-trial-bradley-edwards-wife-witness-row/11741572
108. https://www.watoday.com.au/national/western-australia/claremont-killer-verdict-live-updates-bradley-edwards-fate-to-be-decided-over-deaths-of-sarah-spiers-jane-rimmer-and-ciara-glennon-20200922-p55y3w.html
109. https://www.abc.net.au/news/2020-12-23/claremont-killer-sentenced-for-murders-rape-and-sexual-assault/13007890
110. https://www.watoday.com.au/national/western-australia/wa-police-deny-inaccurate-reports-about-claremont-serial-killer-mistake-20160430-goiyrb.html

111. https://www.abc.net.au/news/programs/
     austory
112. https://www.abc.net.au/news/2020-04-01/
     claremont-serial-killings-edwards-car-fibres-
     matched-victims/12084876
113. https://www.abc.net.au/news/2020-01-29/
     claremont-serial-killings-trial-jane-rimmer-ciara-
     glennon-deaths/11910290
114. https://www.theage.com.au/national/
     gruesome-trail-of-killing-20030909-gdwb7y.html
115. https://www.smh.com.au/national/bodies-in-
     barrels-trial-not-over-20041220-gdkchs.html
116. https://www.smh.com.au/national/bodies-in-
     barrels-trial-not-over-20041220-gdkchs.html
117. https://www.abc.net.au/news/2019-05-20/can-
     snowtown-ever-shake-off-its-dark-past/11082778
118. https://www.smh.com.au/national/chamber-of-
     horrors-20030909-gdhcw0.html
119. https://www.abc.net.au/news/2024-04-17/
     snowtown-murders-accomplice-mark-haydon-
     released/103737300
120. https://journals.sagepub.com/doi/10.1375/
     acri.40.3.249
121. https://www.9news.com.au/national/compo-
     for-carl-williams-daughter/0966f854-8725-4d6e-
     a11d-5fb69b846cca
122. https://www.theage.com.au/national/victoria/
     carl-williams-killed-in-prison-20100419-
     soab.html
123. https://www.heraldsun.com.au/news/victoria/
     pulled-over-en-route-to-prison/news-story/
     9c25f4e8ea2b57041eb23bb510e98eee

124. https://www.heraldsun.com.au/news/special-reports/carl-williams-tells-of-murders/story-e6frf7r6-1111113427917

125. https://www.heraldsun.com.au/news/law-order/how-jason-morans-cold-blooded-murder-made-australia-take-notice-of-the-gangland-wars/news-story/bf872fdc4ff43e5894a38a9881cc5dba

126. https://www.abc.net.au/news/2010-04-19/carl-williams-bashed-and-killed-in-jail/402028

127. Plunkett, Geoff (3 August 2022). *Death Row at Truro*. p. 12. ISBN 978-1-922765-28-4

128. https://www.simonandschuster.com.au/books/Death-Row-at-Truro/Geoff-Plunkett/9781922765291

129. https://www.adelaidenow.com.au/truro-killer-james-miller-died-of-liver-failure-sa-coroners-court-told/story-e6frea6u-1225869567735

130. https://trove.nla.gov.au/newspaper/article/13885882

131. https://records-primo.hosted.exlibrisgroup.com/primo-explore/fulldisplay?context=L&vid=61SRA&lang=en_US&docid=INDEX2059987

132. https://trove.nla.gov.au/newspaper/article/111022290

133. https://trove.nla.gov.au/newspaper/article/13886199

134. https://trove.nla.gov.au/newspaper/article/13890455

135. https://trove.nla.gov.au/newspaper/article/135902960

136. https://www.bailii.org/uk/cases/UKPC/1893/1893_56.html
137. https://trove.nla.gov.au/newspaper/article/13921859
138. https://trove.nla.gov.au/newspaper/article/13925954/1373407
139. https://trove.nla.gov.au/newspaper/article/113320602

About the Author

Alan R Warren is a Bestselling Author, Producer, and host of the popular NBC Radioshow *House of Mystery* and *Inside Writing*, both heard on the 106.5 F.M. Los Angeles/102.3 F.M. Riverside/ 1050 A.M. Palm Springs/ 540 A.M. KYAH Salt Lake City/  1150 A.M. KKNW Seattle/Tacoma and Phoenix.

His bestselling true crime books in Canada include *Beyond Suspicion: The True Story of Colonel Russell Williams*, which will be featured on CNN's *Lies, Crimes, & Videos* (Season 4), and *Murder Times Six: The True Story of the Wells Gray Park Murders*. In America, his bestsellers include *The Killing Game: Serial Killer Rodney Alcala*, which was featured on several television shows such as *Very Scary People with Donny Walberg*, Oxygen's *Mark of a Killer*, Reelz' *Killer Trophies*, and soon to be included in a four-part Sundance Channel documentary called *Death's Date*. His bestseller, *Doomsday Cults: The Devil's Hostages*, was featured on Vice's *Dark Side of the '90s*.

His latest series, *Killer Queens*, is a six-part book series covering murders that affect the Gay Community. So far, it includes Book 1 - Leopold & Loeb, Book 2 - Butcher of Hanover: Fritz Haarmann, Book 3 - Grindr Serial Killer: Stephen Port, and Book 4 - Bruce McArthur: Toronto Gay Killer.

Also By Alan R. Warren

Murderous Minds — United Kingdom

The *International Serial Killers Encyclopedia* series sheds light on the murderous minds of many killers, including their motivations, methods, and madness, through detailed research and explicit retelling of events. Some are notorious names that echo through history books, while others are lesser-known killers whose stories are no less harrowing. Each volume reveals a new layer of darkness.

Monstrous Minds United Kingdom delves into the dark histories of the UK's most infamous murderers from the Victorian era to the present day, as well as some of the lesser-known but equally terrifying criminals. With his signature narrative style, Warren brings to life the twisted minds and heinous acts of killers who have left an indelible mark on British criminal history. His gripping accounts not only recount the gruesome details of their crimes but also offer insights into the psychological, social, and cultural factors that shaped these murderers.

Murderous Minds United Kingdom is more than just a collection of crime stories; it is an exploration of the dark corners of human nature and the enduring fascination with the macabre. Perfect for true crime enthusiasts, historians, and anyone captivated by the complexities of the human mind, this volume is a must-have addition to your bookshelf. Join Alan R. Warren as he unravels the mysteries behind these murderous minds, offering a chilling reminder of the evil that can lurk behind ordinary facades.

Murderous Minds – France

The *International Serial Killers Encyclopedia* series sheds light on the murderous minds of many killers, including their motivations, methods, and madness, through detailed research and explicit retelling of events. Some are notorious names that echo through history books, while others are lesser-known killers whose stories are no less harrowing.

Each volume reveals a new layer of darkness.

Monstrous Minds France, Volume 3, takes you deep into the twisted psyches of France's most notorious serial killers. From the grisly scenes of their crimes to the psychological profiles that unravel their motives, this book offers a chilling exploration of evil incarnate. Each chapter unveils a new horror story, detailing the lives, deeds, and capture of these monstrous individuals who left a trail of fear across the French landscape.

Through meticulous research and compelling narratives, Monstrous Minds France sheds light on the darkness within, leaving readers haunted by the complex web of human depravity and the enduring quest for justice.

Murderous Minds – Soviet Union

The *International Serial Killers Encyclopedia* series sheds light on the murderous minds of many killers, including their motivations, methods, and madness, through detailed research and explicit retelling of events. Some are notorious names that echo through history books, while others are lesser-known killers whose stories are no less harrowing. Each volume reveals a new layer of darkness.

Volume 2 of the series focuses on the most notorious

serial killers from the Soviet Union Era of history. In the shadows of the Iron Curtain, amidst the turmoil of revolution and the rigid structures of the Soviet regime, a different kind of darkness lurked. Behind closed doors and beneath the watchful eyes of the state, a breed of killers emerged, their crimes shrouded in secrecy and fear from the haunting corridors of Moscow to the desolate landscapes of Siberia.

From Andrei Chikatilo, a.k.a. the "Butcher of Rostov," whose insatiable hunger for violence claimed the lives of dozens, leaving a trail of mutilation and terror in his wake, to Vasili Komaroff, a.k.a. the "Wolf of Moscow," who killed so many men, he couldn't even remember his kill count. Each chapter reveals the brutal tales of individuals consumed by their darkest desires and a compelling blend of true crime and psychological intrigue.

Murderous Minds Soviet Union delves deeper, revealing the many enigmatic figures who haunted a nation's collective consciousness. Each chapter unveils a new layer of horror and intrigue where the echoes of the past continue to reverberate to this day.

Murderous Minds – Germany

The *International Serial Killers Encyclopedia* series sheds light on the murderous minds of many killers, including their motivations, methods, and madness, through detailed research and explicit retelling of events. Some are notorious names that echo through history books, while others are lesser-known killers whose stories are no less harrowing. Each volume reveals a new layer of darkness.

Volume 1 of the series focuses on the most notorious serial killers from Germany. It contains many cases where the twisted minds and deeds of those who stalked the streets of Germany left a trail of fear and destruction in their wake.

From the infamous Fritz Haarmann, a.k.a. the "Butcher of Hanover," who preyed upon young boys with chilling brutality, to Peter Kürten, a.k.a. the "Vampire of Dusseldorf," whose thirst for blood knew no bounds. Each chapter reveals the brutal tales of individuals consumed by their darkest desires and a compelling blend of true crime and psychological intrigue.

Murderous Minds Germany offers a chilling glimpse into the darkest recesses of the human psyche, reminding us that evil can lurk just beneath the surface, even in the most civilized society.

MURDER TIMES SIX: The True Story of The Wells Park Murders

"The author even had me (who conducted the interview) on the edge of my seat as I was turning the pages as "the Detective" was trying to unearth the unspeakable truth."

Sgt. Mike Eastham R.C.M.P.

It was a crime unlike anything seen in British Columbia. The horror of the "Wells Gray Murders" almost forty years ago transcends decades.

On August 2, 1982, three generations of a family set out on a camping trip – Bob and Jackie Johnson, their two daughters, Janet, 13 and Karen, 11, and Jackie's parents, George and Edith Bentley. A month later, the

Johnson family car was found off a mountainside logging road near Wells Gray Park completely burned out. In the back seat were the incinerated remains of four adults, and in the trunk were the two girls.

But this was not just your average mass murder. It was much worse. Over time, some brutal details were revealed; however, most are still only known to the murderer, David Ennis (formerly Shearing). His crimes had far-reaching impacts on the family, community, and country. It still does today. Every time Shearing attempts freedom from the parole board, the grief is triggered as everyone is forced to relive the horrors once again.

Murder Times Six shines a spotlight on the crime that captured the attention of a nation, recounts the narrative of a complex police investigation, and discusses whether a convicted mass murderer should ever be allowed to leave the confines of an institution. Most importantly, it tells the story of one family forever changed.

Beyond Suspicion: Russell Williams – A Canadian Serial Killer

Young girl's panties started to go missing; sexual assaults began to occur, and then female bodies were found! Soon this quiet town of Tweed, Ontario, was in a panic. What is even more shocking was when an upstanding resident stood accused of the assaults. This was not just any man, but a pillar of the community; a decorated military pilot who had flown Canadian Forces VIP aircraft for dignitaries such as the Queen of England, Prince Philip, the Governor-General and Prime Minister of Canada.

This is the story of serial killer Russell Williams, the elite pilot of Canada's Air Force One, and the innocent victims he murdered. Unlike other serial killers, Williams seemed very unaffected about his crimes and leading two different lives.

Alan R. Warren describes the secret life including the abductions, rape, and murders that were unleashed on an unsuspecting community. Included are letters written to the victims by Williams and descriptions of the assaults and rapes as seen on videos and photos taken by Williams during the attacks.

This updated version also contains the full brilliant police interrogation of Williams and his confession. Also, the twisted way the Williams planned to pin his crimes on his unsuspecting neighbor.

Doomsday Cults: The Devil's Hostages

Jim Jones convinced his 1000 followers they would all have to commit suicide since he was going to die. Shoko Asahara convinced his followers to release a weapon of mass destruction, the deadly sarin gas, on a Tokyo subway. The Order of the Solar Temple lured the rich and famous, including Princess Grace of Monaco, and convinced them to die a fiery death now on Earth to be reborn on a better planet called Sirius. Charles Manson convinced his followers to kill, in an attempt to incite an apocalyptic race war.

These are a few of the doomsday cults examined in this book by bestselling author Alan R. Warren. Its focus is on cults whose destructive behavior was due in large part to their apocalyptic beliefs or doomsday movements. It includes details surrounding the massacres and a look into how their members became so brainwashed they committed unimaginable crimes at the command of their leader.

Usually, when we hear about these cults and their massacres, we ask ourselves how it possibly happened. We could also ask ourselves, what then is the difference between a cult and a religion? We once had a small group of people who unquestionably followed a person who believed he was the son of God. Two thousand years later, that following is one of the most recognized religions in the world. This book in no way criticizes believing in God. Rather, it examines how a social movement grows into a full religion and when it does not. And what makes the conventional faiths such as Christianity, Judaism, Islam, and Hinduism stand above groups such as the Branch Davidians or Children of God.

In Chains: The Dangerous World of Human Trafficking

Human trafficking is the trade of people for forced labor or sex. It also includes the illegal extraction of human organs and tissues. And it is an extremely ruthless and dangerous industry plaguing our world today.

Most believe human trafficking occurs in countries with no human rights legislation. This is a myth. All types of human trafficking are alive and well in most of the developed countries of the world, like the United States, Canada, and the UK. It is estimated that $150 billion a year is generated in the forced labor industry alone. It is also believed that 21 million people are trapped in modern-day slavery – exploited for sex, labor, or organs.

Most also believe since they live in a free country, there is built-in protection against such illegal practices. But for many, this is not the case. Traffickers tend to focus on the most vulnerable in our society, but trafficking can happen to anyone. You will see how easy it can happen in the stories included in "In Chains."

BUTCHER OF HANOVER: Fritz Haarmann (Killer Queens 2)

Killer Queens is a new series of historical fiction books based on true stories. Sources, such as police reports and newspaper articles, are examined to gather as many facts as possible surrounding each case. As with any work of fiction, some creative additions are made when telling these stories, usually within the conversations between the personalities involved. The various sources are the basis of these conversations and hopefully, make them come alive for the readers to help understand what was meant by those words.

Book 2 of the series focuses on the serial killer of at least twenty-seven young men and boys in Germany in the post-World War I era. At the center of this murder case were Fritz Haarmann and Hans Grans, who were lovers while committing these murders. It wasn't until the skulls and bones started washing ashore from the Leine River in Hanover that Germany realized they had a cold-blooded serial killer in their country.

Unlike Leopold and Loeb murder case covered in Book 1, where the dominance shifted from one to the other, Fritz Haarmann was the dominant partner in this case. He carried out each of the murders and dismemberment of the bodies himself, even though he claimed that Grans chose who was to be murdered in court.

As you read the exploration of the case in this book, ask yourself, did Haarmann murder each victim to keep his lover Hans Grans to stay with him? Did Grans decide who it was that was to be murdered? The evidence on this case will keep you on the edge of your seat, trying to determine who was really behind these gruesome murders.

www.ingramcontent.com/pod-product-compliance
Lightning Source LLC
Chambersburg PA
CBHW070919120626
46546CB00001B/326